NORTH CAROLINA
STATE BOARD OF COMMUNITY COLLEGES
LIBRARIES
STANLY COMMUNITY COLLEGE

CONTEMPORARY
AMERICAN
FICTION

CONTEMPORARY AMERICAN FICTION

by
Nick Hornby

VISION PRESS · LONDON
ST. MARTIN'S PRESS · NEW YORK

Vision Press Ltd.
28 Phillimore Walk
Kensington
London W8 7SA

and

St. Martin's Press, Inc.
175 Fifth Avenue
New York
N.Y. 10010

ISBN (UK) 0 85478 177 3
ISBN (US) 0 312 04213 2

A catalogue record for this book is available
from the British Library

Library of Congress Cataloging-in-Publication Data
Hornby, Nick.
　Contemporary American Fiction/ by Nick Hornby.
　(Critical studies series)
　ISBN 0-312-04213-2
　1. American fiction—20th century—History and criticism.
I. Title.　　II. Series.
PS379.H67　　1991
813'.5409—dc20　　　　　　　　　　　　　　　　　　　91-17979
　　　　　　　　　　　　　　　　　　　　　　　　　　　　　CIP

© 1992 by Nick Hornby
First published in the U.S.A. 1992

All rights reserved

Printed and bound in Great Britain by
Billing & Sons, Worcester.
Typeset by Galleon Photosetting,
Ipswich, Suffolk.
MCMLCII

Contents

		page
1	The *New Yorker* Short Story	7
2	Raymond Carver	30
3	Anne Tyler	53
4	Bobbie Ann Mason	74
5	Richard Ford	93
6	Jayne Anne Phillips; Joy Williams	116
7	Tobias Wolff	133
8	André Dubus	151
	Index	165

1
The *New Yorker* Short Story

> They were as mysterious as cells seen under a microscope; it was difficult not to study them, because they shimmered, flashing for a split second, and then they resumed their shape.
> —Ann Beattie, 'Janus'[1]

This essay will discuss three writers—Ann Beattie, Elizabeth Tallent and Tama Janowitz—who have become associated with the *New Yorker* magazine, and whose stories seem to me to illustrate certain strands that run through contemporary American short fiction; and a fourth, Lorrie Moore, who has made interesting additions to the form, if not the content, of the genre.

In many ways Ann Beattie's short fiction typifies the *New Yorker* story (nine of the fifteen tales in her collection *Where You'll Find Me* were published in that magazine). Elusive, muted, essentially undramatic in their content, their endings consist of the 'infinitesimal shifts in consciousness' that according to one critic characterize Bobbie Ann Mason's fiction; they focus on such tiny slivers of human experience that the quotation which opens this chapter seems to summarize their entire *modus operandi*.

In Ann Beattie's typically thoughtful and temperate introduction to *The Best American Short Stories, 1987*, her comments on Madison Smartt Bell's contribution provide an unconscious insight into her own work:

> This year, I read [Bell's] story with fascination and dread, simultaneously tantalized by the events and as done-in as the character by their implications. It was like being on a roller coaster. I had to enjoy the ride I was being taken on, but at the same time it shook me up a little too much.[2]

It would be easy from this to cast Beattie as some latter-day Jane Austen, with a narrow range centring on the lives and loves of the middle class, and appalled by the squalor and danger of 'real life'. (Smartt Bell's story is a typically bleak slice of New York low-life.) Yet novels such as *Picturing Will* and *Love Always*, with their unexpected and occasionally sharp intrusions of pain and sexuality and violence, suggest that an accusation of isolation would be unfair. In the introduction Beattie goes on to say that 'Other times, the writer's timing was perfect', and it becomes clear that it is the violence of Bell's story-telling that disturbs her, rather than the violence inherent in the world he portrays. For Beattie, too much happens, too quickly.

Nobody could make the same accusation of her own minimalist narratives. 'Janus', the story quoted above, is about a woman's obsession with a bowl; 'In the White Night' describes a couple's journey home from a dinner party. It is highly unlikely that a Beattie reader will ever complain of feeling too shaken up. Yet the stories work on a number of levels, and represent state-of-the-art sophistication of the minute observations that have recently characterized U.S. short fiction.

The understatement and apparent slightness of Beattie's work is such that some of the stories operate more on the level of poetry than narrative, with one central image providing a clue to meanings that would otherwise remain obscure. 'Skeletons', for example, is an impressionistic and deceptively random portrait of three young people who share a house. Nancy and Garrett, both artists, are lovers; Kyle, the youngest of the three, is beginning to feel isolated by the intimacy of the couple. The bulk of the narrative—and the story is less than six pages long—takes place over the space of a few minutes. Nancy and Garrett are about to embrace when Kyle interrupts them to inform them that he has prepared their supper. The last two paragraphs consist of a flash-forward: Nancy and Garrett are now married, and Nancy is unhappy and frustrated, no longer drawing, no longer in love. They have lost touch with Kyle, who suddenly has a vision of Nancy when his car goes into a skid.

The title refers superficially to this quasi-mystical ending

The 'New Yorker' Short Story

(we are shown Garrett and Nancy out trick-or-treating on Halloween, and Nancy is wearing a skeleton suit), but its real relevance is to be found earlier on:

> Kyle had once told Nancy, on one of their late-fall walks, that one of his fears had been that someone might be able to read his mind. It was clear to her that he had fantasies about them. At the time, Nancy had tried to pass it off lightly; she told them that when she was drawing she always sensed the model's bones and muscles, and what she did was stroke a soft surface over them until a body took form.[3]

'Skeletons' turns on this metaphor. Nancy's oblique remark is designed to reassure Kyle that the transparency he fears is not threatening, but her words also contain a truth about the process of self-knowledge (we are told that Nancy is seeing a psychologist in the first part of the story), a capacity that she would appear to have lost along with her determination to draw.

It is an impressively complex story, but the real point here is its exemplification of the miniaturist (as opposed to minimalist) school of writing that the *New Yorker* favours. Hence the bowl in 'Janus': it is almost as if Beattie's express intention is to sharpen her focus so that she is capable of finding resonance in the most banal of domestic details. In Bill Buford's introduction to *Granta 8: Dirty Realism*, he argues that Ann Beattie (not included in the collection) shares 'many of the same assumptions about language, character and narrative'[4] as Carver, Wolff, Jayne Anne Phillips *et al.*, but it is difficult to make much of a case for this assertion. It is not just that Beattie's world contains none of the harshnesses found in that of the Dirty Realists; there is an unwillingness to deal with major themes head-on.

Like Carver's 'A Small, Good Thing', Tyler in *The Accidental Tourist* and Ford in *The Sportswriter*, Beattie's 'In the White Night' deals with the death of a child, or rather the interminable aftermath of such a tragedy. It is, inevitably, a beautiful story, and Beattie's miniaturism is predictably suited to an examination of the gestures that accompany coping: 'In the White Night' ends with the long-since bereaved parents asleep in their living room, father on the sofa and mother on the floor. ('In the white night world outside, their daughter might be drifting past like an angel, and she would see this tableau, for the second that she hovered, as a necessary small adjustment.'[5]) There is a sense in which the absence of pain directly expressed is the whole point of the story, but it is difficult to imagine many of the writers in the *Granta* collection settling for the delicacy—of language, of theme, even—that characterizes Beattie's work. Conversely, Beattie's characters—comfortably middle-class, invariably suburban—would find very little in common with the alienated narrators of Ford's *Rock Springs* and Wolff's 'The Barracks Thief'.

If Beattie cannot really be regarded in the same light as her realist contemporaries, then the lesser-known Elizabeth Tallent would on the face of it seem to share many more characteristics. Her short story 'Why I Love Country Music' does feature in *Granta 8*, and its opening paragraph contains a startlingly detailed account of a cattle castration, as well as an introduction to the narrator's boy-friend, a diminutive miner named Nod who likes to go dancing in cowboy bars. It is easy to see why Buford fell upon the story:

> Sometimes, living in the desert, you understand the need for an elaborate code of ritual laws; without them, the desert makes you an accomplice in all kinds of graceless crimes.[6]

Sentences like this—and Tallent's story is studded with them—give the promise of the kind of low-life veracity that the editor seems to be looking for.

The opening of 'Grant of Easement', the first story in Tallent's collection *Time with Children*, however ('The magpies were drawn to construction. There was something piratical in their black eyes and intent, lilting flight'[7]), suggests a somewhat different set of preoccupations, and in fact much of the book, the majority of which first appeared in the *New Yorker*, is highly reminiscent of Beattie's work. This is surprising, given the style and content of 'Why I Love Country Music', with its frank explorations of sexuality, its clever, challenging use of metaphor and above all its blue collar setting. Duncan Webster used Tallent's early work, of which the latter is an example, to illustrate the strengths in the new American fiction:

> There is also the ease with which writers like Elizabeth Tallent or Tobias Wolff can move from representing cowboy bars to faculty meetings, from car salesmen to architectural engineers. Reading this fiction in Britain where novelists seem to have carved out small territories of specialization (High Church society or middle-aged woman academics in North Oxford or disillusioned journalists in Islington, and so on) this mobility is one of the most refreshing features of the writing.[8]

There is really no sign of this mobility in *Time with Children*, however. It is populated by the urbane middle-class professionals that Beattie favours: one group of four linked stories, for example, takes place in London, where a young American publisher, Charlie, is on secondment. The transatlantic setting is very interesting in the light of Webster's observations; suddenly, Tallent's work has stopped resembling that of Tobias Wolff and started to take on the air of some of the English writers Webster alludes to above. Tallent's London is actually startlingly similar to the London of Kingsley Amis or Penelope Lively; the occasional stab at observation of the modern city ('with his worn Levi's, scuffed leather jacket and close-cropped fair head, Brian could have been a rough American kid, even a gang member. This was a London ideal...'[9]) is offset by the inexplicable lapses into the world of Conan Doyle. The elderly English couple from whom Charlie and his wife have rented a flat ('seven cheerless Edwardian rooms'[10]) have gone to South Africa; when Nicholas, Charlie's young son, develops a stealing habit, we are told that he has taken a farthing from his baby-sitter. Why she should have a farthing in her handbag remains unclear.

Obviously Tallent is on unfamiliar territory, and thus unable to capture London entirely authentically, but given that (as Webster argues) contemporary American writing draws a great deal of its freshness from its authenticity, these false notes could arguably be taken as an indicator that the writer has moved away from the *Granta* group and into the *New Yorker* main stream. This is not to say, of course, that the Beattie school is unreliable, or unobservant; it is not. I am merely drawing attention to these anachronistic touches to show that authenticity has ceased to be a priority. One reason why, say, Bobbie Ann Mason has yet to set a story outside Kentucky is that she would suddenly be unable to fix her characters into a time and place with such exactitude (Mason's references to TV and music, as I have discussed, are particularly important to her; *In Country* is set very clearly in the summer of 1984). Beattie's quartet of London stories contains one reference to Mrs. Thatcher, but beyond that her themes—marriage and adultery, the relationship between parents and children—strive for 'timelessness', if such a quality is ever attainable in fiction.

Tallent's movement towards a mainstream of American magazine short-story writing is not unique. The many strengths of Lorrie Moore's writing are discussed elsewhere in this chapter, but it is worth noting here that her second volume of short stories, *Like Life*, contains very little of the stylistic innovation—the use of the imperative or the second-person forms for narration, for example—that distinguished her first, *Self-Help*. Tallent's early work showed little sign of any such desire to challenge the accepted parameters of the medium in this way (although in *Time with Children* the 'surprising, often surreal images'[11] that Webster refers to are in short supply). It is her 'mobility' that has vanished, and though the four London stories, together with a second quartet set in New Mexico, do exemplify Tallent's ability to take the reader into worlds outside New York and Connecticut, the perspective has changed: the mobility here is that of the affluent middle-class woman, rather than that of the writer tired of the narrow range of contemporary fiction. Only in 'No-one's a Mystery' and 'Two Ghosts of Us', in which a battered woman makes love to her old high school sweetheart before returning to her husband, does Tallent remind the reader why Buford saw fit to include her alongside Ford, Carver and the rest.

The stories of Tama Janowitz and Lorrie Moore illustrate a different trend in American fiction. It was a trend initiated by the success of *Bright Lights, Big City*, Jay McInerney's sharp, well-written novel portraying the fashionable *demi-monde* of young middle-class New Yorkers: in the second half of the '80s Janowitz, Moore, Bret Easton Ellis, Susan Minot, Gary Indiana (whose novel *Horse Crazy* is the darkest of the genre) and others produced novels or collections of short stories which appear imitative of or inspired by McInerney's book.

The central character in *Bright Lights, Big City* (first published in 1984)—effectively the narrator, although McInerney uses the second person throughout the book—works for a smart, stuffy and prestigious New York magazine as a fact-checker. His predilection for cocaine and night-clubs, however, eventually makes his position at the magazine untenable; jobless and wifeless, he finally learns to confront the central incident in his life, the loss of his mother.

The novel is, unsurprisingly, very attentive to the surfaces of fashionable New York—the language, the drugs, the music, the clubs—and McInerney has a pleasingly acute eye for the absurdity of it all. What is particularly noticeable here, however, is that *Bright Lights, Big City* is a curiously homely book: if the central character had managed to stay married, it seems to be saying, and if he had managed to face his mother's death at an earlier stage, then he would not find it necessary to spend his salary on cocaine. This central core of domestic longing, as we shall see, is echoed in Tama Janowitz's work.

Slaves of New York, Janowitz's début, consists of a series of interlocking short stories. (This format was also used by Susan Minot, in *Monkeys*, and Karen Karbo, in *Trespassers Welcome Here*.) The stories are set in the world of New York's artistic community: Stash and Marley are painters, narrator Eleanor designs jewellery, Victor is a dealer, and so on. Those who have kept abreast of the wave of 'brat pack' fiction published in the States over the last few years will be familiar with the milieu, as the art world has served as a backdrop to Indiana's *Horse Crazy* and occasional stories in Susan Minot's second collection, *Lust*, among other recent books. The literary world's fascination with the visual arts is puzzling at first; after all, even in New York artists form a tiny community, and Janowitz's presentation of them as the centre of the fashionable universe is hard to understand, given the competition from film-makers, writers and musicians. It would appear that artists essentially serve as a trope in these works: given the writer's understandable reluctance to write about writing (and the reluctance of publishers to accept works of this kind), Janowitz and Co. have found an acceptable alternative in painters and sculptors and photographers. Artist and writer both operate in isolation, and both work in areas in which it is notoriously difficult to make any kind of living, thus providing opportunities for plenty of colourful descriptions of cockroach-infested lofts. Perhaps more crucially, writers and artists both tend to regard themselves as nonconformist.

Slaves of New York begins in a shockingly memorable fashion. The first sentence of the first story, 'Modern Saint #271' (Janowitz is fond of the modish and meaningless numberings) runs as follows: 'After I became a prostitute, I had to deal with penises of every imaginable shape and size.'[12] The only observations to be made here about this story—a rather thin account of how a bright Jewish girl ended up street-walking—are that it was not, unlike several others from the collection, first published in the *New Yorker*; and that it is entirely unrepresentative of the main body of the book. Why it has been placed quite so prominently at the front of the book remains a matter for conjecture.

The collection features several stories outlining the progress of narrator Eleanor, a young jewellery designer, and her relationship with her moody artist boy-friend Stash. Eleanor is in sharp contrast to the narrator of 'Modern Saint #271'; she is a little dizzy, and almost wilfully passive:

> In the morning I clean up some, I walk his Dalmation, Andrew, then I come back and cook Stash two poached eggs, raisin tea biscuits, coffee with three spoons sugar. . . I watch a few soap operas and have a second cup. Then usually I plan the evening dinner.[13]

There is, of course, a high degree of satirical intent in the Eleanor stories; and yet Janowitz apparently intends her readers to allow an equal amount of affectionate identification with her central character. Eleanor is witty and charming, although this wit is usually articulated non-verbally—in her designs, for instance: 'I worked in rubber, shellacked sea-horses, plastic James Bond-doll earrings.'[14] This kind of parody of the *au courant* trash aesthetic would inevitably have provoked knowing chuckles from a certain section of readership, and yet these are chuckles of recognition rather than derision, as in a sense Eleanor's jewellery is already a form of satire.

Similarly, the character's frequent references to her dress sense are apparently designed to strengthen this recognition. In 'The Slaves in New York', she describes her glasses, 'which were pointy, and had little rhinestones in the corners',[15] and her coat, 'Day-Glo orange wool with a green velvet collar'[16]; in 'Patterns' she mentions a 'silver coat'[17] and an 'orange mini-dress with a peace symbol cut out over the stomach'.[18] Clothes, then, are important to Eleanor as self-expression, and to Janowitz as a series of signals to the reader. Yet if the writer's purpose here is not wholly satirical, then the Eleanor stories are, at bottom, as reassuring as the conclusion of *Bright Lights, Big City*.

The title of the book suggests a group of characters who are in thrall to the vibrancy of the city; and yet it is taken from a story entitled 'The Slaves in New York', the story which introduces us to Eleanor, and the phrase refers not to young, penniless bohemians but to women. It occurs when Eleanor is trying to give some advice to a friend from Boston who has been invited to live with an 'old flame' in New York.

> I said, 'Abby, don't do it. In the old days, marriages were arranged by the parents, and maybe you ended up with a jerk but at least you had the security of marriage, no one could dump you out on the street. In today's world, it's the slave system. If you live with this guy in New York, you'll be the slave.'[19]

Eleanor's preoccupation with marriage is reiterated in 'Patterns', when she listens to a man at a dinner party assert that 'all the women I know are just as obsessed with Lane Hope chests and *Bride* magazine as if it was the 1950s'. The other guests look to Eleanor to respond; 'but I didn't have anything else to say.'[20] At the conclusion of the story, Eleanor visits a bookshop:

> I bought four books: Dale Carnegie's 'How to Stop Worrying and Start Living'; a book on transactional analysis to write your own life script; 'How to Make a Man Marry You in Thirty Days; and something on reincarnation.[21]

Obviously this conclusion is comic. But what, precisely, is the joke? It would appear to be that the aspirations of the central character, despite her membership of the young New York art set, despite the orange mini-dress with the peace symbol cut into it, are really very ordinary; Janowitz is not talking to her own kind here (after all, the Eleanor stories were serialized in the staid *New Yorker* rather than one of its more fashionable rivals) but to a middle-class readership who are aware of the bohemian crowd but know nothing about them. Don't worry, the author is saying; Eleanor is really no different to the rest of you.

It is noticeable in *Slaves of New York* that Janowitz's emphasis elsewhere is different. 'You and the Boss' (which first appeared in the rock magazine *Spin*) is a parody of the myth that has been built around Bruce Springsteen; 'Kurt and Natasha, a Relationship' (which first appeared in *Interview*) is a self-consciously bizarre account of a self-consciously perverse liaison. *Slaves of New York* is an uneven collection because its genesis in different magazines has not allowed its author any kind of consistent perspective on its characters; at bottom the Eleanor stories are Ann Beattie's miniatures dressed in day-glo, and fit uneasily into the rest of the collection.

It is perhaps unsurprising that Lorrie Moore should have been praised for her freshness of style, her vitality, her uniqueness. Given the relentless uniformity of much recent American short fiction, the stylistic tricks of Moore's first collection *Self-Help* (first published in 1985) help to separate the writer from many of her peers; those who have taken a keen interest in the form, however, will recognize that Moore's methods do contain echoes of earlier American women authors, even if her eclecticism and her magpie-like methods of working create a genuinely unusual voice.

Moore's themes—love, loneliness, the relationships between mother and child—are familiar enough, as is their urban or suburban setting. Indeed, they are so familiar that her particular version of the urban woman—sad, wryly witty, either involved in a disastrous relationship or desperately looking for some kind of partner—has achieved the status of urban myth. It has long been the staple diet of films and televisions: the '70s' TV series *Rhoda*, for example, featured a central character who was an unreconstructed embodiment of this idea; the films of Woody Allen frequently centre around Urban Woman, and the part that Allen plays, particularly in his comedies, is a direct male equivalent. The central weakness in *Self-Help* is that Moore makes no attempt to examine or reappraise the myth, which has perhaps been exhausted by now; what is interesting about her work, however, is the complexity she brings to the innate sentimentality of the genre.

The first story, 'How to Be an Other Woman', serves as a perfect introduction to the predominant voice in the book. Like several of the stories ('How to Become a Writer', 'How to Talk to Your Mother (Notes)', 'The Kid's Guide to Divorce' and, simply, 'How') the story is written either in the imperative voice or in the second person, and thus reads like a quirky parody of the pop psychological best sellers alluded to in the title of the collection. 'How to Be an Other Woman' purports to be a guide to having an affair with a married man:

> Slip carefully out, like a shoe horn, from beneath his sleeping body—he grunts groggily—and go to the closet. Open it with a minimum of squeaking and stare at her clothes. A few suits. . . . Look at the shoes. They are all lined up in neat, married pairs on the closet floor. . . . They have been to an expensive college, say, in Massachusetts.[22]

The tone of the 'advice' proffered here is set by the quotations Moore uses as a preface to the book, which are taken from works entitled *Sex Lives of Animals Without*

Backbones, *The Amy Vanderbilt Complete Guide to Etiquette* (this last quotation deals with the problem of shaking hands with an amputee) and *Butchering Livestock at Home*; the self-help Moore recommends is similarly grisly, and her source material indicative of the uneasy humour found throughout the stories. Yet it is their fragmentary nature, as much as their comic tone, that distinguishes them; in 'How to Be an Other Woman' the narrative is disrupted by lists (of ex-lovers, needs, the contents of an alien medicine chest); 'How to Talk to Your Mother (Notes)' is written in a kind of annual diary form, commencing in 1982 and working back to the narrator's birth in 1939. Moore takes considerable pains to prevent her stories from lapsing into *New Yorker*-style conventionality; paradoxically it is this straining for new fictional forms that makes her stories reminiscent of another, earlier exponent of short fiction.

> On first meeting [her] work the reader is conscious of hearing an entirely new voice—a strange, brief, intermittent yet fluent voice, which tells in fragments of stories, or stories within stories, a discontinuous tale of American urban struggle.[23]

Thus wrote A. S. Byatt in 1979 (six years before the publication of Moore's first collection), of Grace Paley, who was born in 1922 but has published only a handful of short-story collections. Paley's work is more abstruse, more complex, than Moore's; but Byatt's observations are still interestingly apposite here, and occasional phrases—she refers to the 'scatty muddling-through vitality'[24] and the 'rotten rosy temperaments'[25] of Paley's characters—will strike chords with those familiar with Moore's work.

Certainly Paley operates on similar thematic territory, and uses a similarly sardonic tone of voice. Her three-page story 'Wants' begins as follows:

> I saw my ex-husband in the street. I was sitting on the steps of the new library.
> Hello, my life, I said. We had once been married for twenty-seven years, so I felt justified.
> He said, What? What life? No life of mine.[26]

Compare this with the following passage from Moore's 'Amahl and the Night Visitors':

> He doesn't understand that you've planned your lives together. That you have even planned your deaths together, not really deaths at all but more like a *pas de deux*. Like Gene Kelly and Leslie Caron in *An American in Paris*, only older.[27]

Paley's prose is less jocular, but there is an equivalent dead-pan style; in a sense Lorrie Moore is Grace Paley filtered through twenty years of TV sitcom, and the cultural references that each writer uses underline this. In 'Wants' the narrator is returning to the library two books by Edith Wharton, the proto-feminist writer, *The Children* and *The House of Mirth* (which A. S. Byatt describes as 'a gallant female novel about failure'[28]); in 'How to Be an Other Woman' the narrator is reading ' "Madame Bovary" in a Doris Day biography jacket'.[29] (Throughout the stories, and in her novel *Anagrams*, Moore shows an alarming preoccupation with the trashiest of Hollywood musicals (*Thoroughly Modern Millie*, *The Turning Point*): her pop cultural references are studiedly ersatz.) Moore is making explicit not only the ambiguous ambitions of her narrator (a college graduate who works as a typist) but the cultural schizophrenia that distinguishes both her characters and her fiction.

Another interesting point of comparison is that both writers directly address the contradictions that arise in their work. In 'A Conversation with my Father' Paley confronts her own savagely pared prose. The narrator is trying to construct a story according to her dying father's tastes: he wants her to write

> a simple story just once more . . . the kind de Maupassant wrote, or Chekhov. The kind you used to write. Just recognizable people and then write down what happened to them next.[30]

The narrator responds with a nine-line story about a mother who becomes a junkie in order to 'maintain her close friendship' with her son. (In 'Wants', remember, Paley reduces a twenty-seven-year marriage to three pages.) The father complains that she has 'left everything out', and the narrator responds with an expanded but still conventionally inadequate version: this time, the father objects to the fact that his daughter 'can't tell a plain story', but, more importantly, worries about the plight that has befallen the mother at the conclusion of the story. Consequently the story-teller provides him with a series of unlikely happy endings, but these prove equally unsatisfactory: 'Tragedy!' the father cries. 'You too! When will you look it in the face?'[31]

In Byatt's words, 'The truth is, precisely, that she does. This tale . . . tells us Life has no pity and the author has. And hence the passionate/dispassionate, involved, chilly paradox of that voice.'[32] 'A Conversation with my Father' is an extraordinarily complex Chinese box of a story; Paley's analysis of authorial responsibility gives an extra dimension to the rest of the collection, as if she cannot bear the reader to assume that her gloomy disengagement elsewhere represents both her vision (which is bleak) *and* her soul (which is more compassionate).

Lorrie Moore makes a similar, if less ambitious, attempt to contextualize her work in the last story in *Self-Help*, 'To Fill'. The preceding stories—particularly the 'How. .' stories—are studded with an alarming number of puns, some unusual and witty, some stale and weak. 'I suffer indignities at your hands,' says the narrator to her married lover in 'How to Be an Other Woman', 'And agonies of duh feet. I don't know why I joke. I hurt.'[33] It is possible to mistake Moore's intentions here; as I have already argued, the self-deprecatingly witty woman who masks her unhappiness and rejection by joking is a staple of much American comedy, and the relentless punning does sometimes give Moore's stories the appearance of being less complex than they actually are. But in 'To Fill' (whose narrator, Riva, ends up stabbing her adulterous husband Tom in a restaurant) the jokes are given an unexpectedly reflective significance:

> Tom reaches under the covers and clasps my hand. Riva, I'm worried about you. Everything's a joke. You're always flip-flopping words, only listening to the edge of things. It's like you're always, constantly, on the edge.
> Life is a pun, I say. It's something that sounds like one thing but also sounds like even means like something else.

Riva what you just said. It's empty. It doesn't mean anything. He says this with a tender reluctance, as if it were the last thing in the world he wanted to do.[34]

Despite Tom's unsympathetic rôle in the story, his observations here are crucial to an understanding of Moore's female characters, whose occasionally irritating flippancy comes not from a lack of discipline in the writing, but from this tendency to 'listen to the edge of things'. Despite their entirely different background and education and verbal facility, Moore's women suffer from the same sort of aphasia as those of Raymond Carver; their words are inadequate for the circumstances in which they find themselves, and Moore's placing of 'To Fill' at the end of *Self-Help* can be taken as an aid to understanding the collection in its entirety: these stories are about glibness, rather than in themselves glib.

In the 'How. .' stories, language itself serves as a kind of trope—the puns have a metaphorical significance. It is thus pertinent that Moore's novel, *Anagrams*, contains a similar examination of the link between language and the world. Again, Moore's disruption of conventional narrative forms is noteworthy: in *Anagrams* the narrative consists of a series of short stories which centre around the trio of Benna, her friend Eleanor and her friend/lover/neighbour Gerard. Each story is essentially a scrambled version of the basic set-up; thus in the first, Benna is a night-club singer, while Gerard pines hopelessly through the dividing wall; in the second, Benna is an unemployed aerobics teacher who discovers that her lover Gerard has been having an affair with Eleanor, and so on. It is an intriguing progression, but it is entirely typical that Moore should choose for the novel's title, and therefore as a description of this narrative process, a word that itself refers to words and the various meanings contained within them.

It is the quietest, least pyrotechnical story in *Self-Help* that foreshadows Moore's latest work, however. 'What is Seized', an account of the failed marriage of narrator Lynnie's parents, though darker than anything else in the book, still exhibits Moore's fascination with word-play and flippancy: when told at college about her mother's mastectomy, Lynnie recalls that she replied with a note saying 'Was sorry to hear about the hospital thing. Hope you're feeling better. I've got tests by the millions!'[35] Reflecting on these lines, the mature Lynnie remarks:

> I wonder what else I could have written, those winters, looking out and seeing snow lining the elm grove like an arthritis and finding no words. I didn't lie: there were a lot of tests; I had a lot of tests.[36]

In 'What is Seized' Moore finds a voice in which she can pun with sobriety. There are passages in the story where the author's intention is not to entertain and provoke, but to confront and even to appal, and its quasi-feminist starkness is more directly reminiscent of Paley:

> But when [my father] made love to my mother, he kept his eyes closed the whole time, turned his head away from her, and afterward would give her a hard, angry gaze, roll stiffly over to his side of the bed, face the wall, shake her off of him with a shudder or flinch if she kissed his shoulder, rubbed his arm, lay a palm against his bare back. She told me this before she died. She just stared off to one side of the drapes and told me.[37]

Moore does not hit quite this note again in *Like Life*, her second collection; but its echo has remained with her, and several of the stories reveal a similar sense of cool despair. The title of the book, though, is in fact a punch-line to a grim and entirely typical joke. When Mamie, the central character of the title story has a mole removed, the doctor remarks simply ' "Precancer." "Precancer?' she had repeated quietly, for she was a quiet woman. "Isn't that . . . like *life*?" '[38] The phrase is repeated later in the story, when she asks a colleague about her love life: 'I don't have a love life. I have a like life.'[39] Again, the multiplicity of meanings in words is teased out; when Mamie recalls her husbands 'lifelike' impressions of singers and actors, his imitations underline the way that simile and metaphor can have a real, physical existence in Moore's fiction.

The title story is atypical of the collection as a whole: it is a grim, apocalyptic fantasy, a portrait of a crumbling relationship set in a crumbling, disease-ridden city. 'Two Boys', the first story in the book, is both more representative and more successful ('Like Life' is swamped by its futuristic setting: many of Moore's attempts to visualize New York at the end of the current decade are over-familiar from science-fiction books, films and TV programmes), although it underlines Moore's new interest in images of decay, and provides further explorations of her idea that the world contains as many puns as her fiction. The title here refers to its central character's love life ('For the first time in her life, Mary was seeing two boys at once'[40]); she refers to her lovers as 'Number One' and 'Number Two', and creates an imaginary lover, 'Number Three', 'composed of the best features of each':

> It was boy number three, she realized, she desired. Alone, Number One was rich and mean. Number Two was sighing, repetitive, tall, going on forever; you just wanted him to sit down. It was inevitable that she splice and add. One plus two. Three was clever and true.[41]

The ambiguity of the last sentence—does it refer to the name she has invented for her fantasy, or the fantasy figure itself?—is a commonplace in Moore's fiction: here, the neatness of the mathematical construct mirrors and puns on the neatness of the concept of the imaginary figure. Again, the title recurs in a different context: 'You don't know what it's like to have two boys',[42] Number One tells Mary, referring to his sons.

In *Self-Help*, 'Two Boys' might have been given a frivolous, frothy surface, but in *Like Life* a number of disturbing images give the story a hard, dark centre. Mary lives over a meat company:

> She tried not to let the refrigerated smell follow her in the door, up the stairs, the vague shame and hamburger death of it, though sometimes it did. Every day she attempted not to step in the blood that ran off the sidewalk and collected in the gutter, dark and alive.[43]

Mary's attempts to avoid the blood are indicative of her inability to confront her life (we are told that her 'nervous collapse . . . took the form of trips to a small neighbourhood park, for which she dressed all in white: white blouses, white skirts, white anklets, shoes flat and white as boat sails'[44]); but the meat company seems to represent the way that Mary's horror of things beneath the surface has lost all sense of proportion. Her attempt to escape from her situation takes her to Ottowa, 'British and empty'[45]; in her hotel room she imagines 'the cool bridal bleach of the sheets healing her, holding her like a shroud, working their white temporarily through her skin and into the thinking blood of her'.[46] She strives for this antiseptic whiteness as an antidote to the blood that runs in the gutter outside her house, and in a sense neither ambition nor fear is an appropriate response to the actuality.

Moore returns to the meat images at the end of the story. Throughout the story Mary has had encounters with a strange, tough young girl in the park ('Message from outer space', the girl says to Mary after unleashing a ball of spit at her feet[47]), and it is this girl who brings 'Two Boys' to its conclusion:

> The girl stared at the meat displayed in the windows, the phallic harangue of sausages, marbled, dessicated, strung up as for a carnival.
>
> 'Look!' said the girl. 'There they are. All our old boyfriends.'
>
> Mary took off her dark glasses. 'What grade are you in?' she asked. Could there be a grade for what this girl knew in her bulleted heart? What she knew was the sort of thing that grew in you like a tree, unfurling in your brain, pushing out into your fingers against the nails.[48]

'Two Boys' is a sombre, strange, opaque story, and pushes Moore's writing into a new dimension: she has never dealt with this kind of bleak exploration of the subconscious before. The girl's grim observation is, one presumes, delivered with some black levity, but it has a resonant force for Mary, who has been chopping up and discarding pieces of her lovers in order to form a new one; her own immaturity, her unwillingness to face her adulthood (her white clothes are curiously little-girl sexless) is set against this child's dreadful, savage awareness.

'Vissi D'Arte', the second story in the collection, ends on a similarly desperate note. It is an account of a (male) writer's struggle to survive in New York; where Mary lived above a meat company, Harry lives above a sex pavilion. 'He had lived there five years and had never gone in, a fact of which he was proud. In the land of perversities he had maintained the perversity of refusal.'⁴⁹ Much of the story is a Tama Janowitz-style lament to the impossibility of surviving as an artist in the city; Harry loses his girl-friend, his writing is plagiarized by a TV producer, a brown bilge appears through the plumbing in his bath, and so on. What separates the story from much 'brat pack' fiction is the plangency of its final image, which takes 'Vissi D'Arte' into a new and entirely serious area. The story closes with Harry entering the sex pavilion and entering one of the booths, where he watches the gyrations of a naked girl, 'sleepy and indifferent':

> But as he watched she seemed to lift her eyes, to spot him, to head towards his window, slow and smiling, until she was pressing her breast against his pane, his alone. He moaned, placed his mouth against the cold single rose of her nipple, against the hard smeared glass, though given time, in this, this wonderful town, he felt, it might warm beneath his labors, truly, like something real.⁵⁰

Harry is the real slave of New York: desperate, deluded, reduced to pathetic and hopeless gesture by the meanness of the city. And while there is complexity in this image—combining as it does Harry's aborted attempts to prostitute himself (to the TV producer) and his self-delusion—there is no ironic ambiguity. The disturbing nature of the conclusion to 'Vissi D'Arte' is rare in this vein of contemporary American short fiction, in that it is engaged, urgent, undetached, and it is this new capacity to disturb that separates Moore from many of her peers.

Despite the fact that several of the stories in *Like Life* are set in the mid-west, the collection is still very New York-centred. A notion of the city is central to 'You're Ugly, Too' and 'The Jewish Hunter' (both first published in the *New Yorker*). Zoe Hendricks, the central character in the first, is exiled in Illinois ('You had to get out of them occasionally, these Illinois towns with the funny names',⁵¹ the story begins; Zoe goes back to Manhattan, to visit her sister); Odette in 'The Jewish Hunter' is an impoverished New York poet, the beneficiary of a mid-west library fellowship. Both Zoe and Odette are aware of the absence of the city; and while 'You're Ugly, Too', is, like 'Vissi D'Arte', essentially a variation on a commonplace urban theme (this time the alienation of the romantically unattached), 'The Jewish Hunter' is an interesting and rich variation to the *New Yorker* canon.

The story is a strange and allusive account of Odette's affair with a mid-west Jew, Pinky Eliot. The relationship bridges a cultural divide, because ostensibly the couple have very little in common: Pinky tells Odette that her poems are too 'literaturey'[52] for him, Odette hates the food in Pinky's favourite restaurant, Pinky takes Odette hunting (an experience she loathes) and Odette's quick-fire New York cynicism is contrasted with Pinky's flat mid-western mannerisms and conversation. This gulf is emphasized when they visit a local tourist attraction, the Cave of the Many Mounds. The guide turns the light off in the cave so that the visitors can imagine it in its natural state; Odette leans, 'blind and hungry, into his arm'.[53] Later, she writes to friends that 'She had met this guy. Something had happened to the two of them in a cave, she wasn't sure what.'[54]

There is, of course, another book in which something obscure happens between two people from different cultures in a cave when the lights go out: it is the central incident in Forster's *A Passage to India*, and it is impossible to imagine that the scene in 'The Jewish Hunter' is anything but a deliberate allusion. In 'The Jewish Hunter', however, whatever takes place between Pinky and Odette helps them to cement their relationship, and the couple sleep together for the first time immediately afterwards. Here Moore adds another element to the story: after love-making, Pinky habitually watches a videotape entitled 'Holocaust Survivors', and Odette discovers that his parents were killed in the concentration camps. 'Heavy stuff', Pinky remarks after each viewing; 'Who on earth was entitled to such words?',[55] Odette wonders. There is, here, a return to Moore's old obsessions with glibness; but 'The Jewish Hunter' is more a story about how tenderness as a state can form between two people whose depths correspond much more closely than their surfaces. Ultimately Odette remains as elusive to herself as she does to us, and returns to New York feeling like 'someone of whom she was fond, an old and future friend of herself, still unspent and up ahead somewhere, like a light that moves'.[56]

It must be observed that the story is not entirely successful;

The 'New Yorker' Short Story

Odette's flip one-liners introduce a tone that sits uneasily with some of the themes raised, and Moore's ambitions seem too diverse to be fitted comfortably within the confines of the form. Yet it is in 'The Jewish Hunter' and 'Two Boys' that Lorrie Moore suggests she is capable of adding a new layer of possibility and meaning to this particular strain of American short fiction, and that she can thus find a way out of the impasse that it seems to have created for itself.

I have argued here that the *New Yorker* short story—always resolutely domestic—has begun recently to strait-jacket writers like Ann Beattie and Elizabeth Tallent, and has directly influenced both the form and the content of other, younger writers such as Tama Janowitz, who might have been expected to challenge the accepted mode of this kind of short fiction. Lorrie Moore offers a fresh approach, and her particular blend of humour and pain at least distinguishes her from other writers in this group.

It would be unreasonable to expect domestic short fiction of this kind to provide much in the way of experimentation; even the best writers in the illustrious history of the *New Yorker* short story—Cheever and Updike, for example—are hardly renowned for their desire to challenge form, although Raymond Carver's middle-period experiments with a sort of extreme ellipsis offer an interesting alternative to received ideas. Carver, however, is something of an anomaly given his blue-collar characters, and his frequent appearances in the *New Yorker* were a testament more to his influence as a literary figure than to a genuine attempt on the part of the magazine to offer a plurality of styles and backgrounds. There have been recent interesting approaches to portrayals of quotidien middle-class life: the *New Yorker* was an early medium for Nicholson Baker, whose two extraordinary novellas, *The Mezzanine* and *Room Temperature*, take miniaturism to its logical conclusion with their witty contemplations of the drinking straw, the interlocking leaves at the top of escalators, and why and when we are given paper bags in shops. And David Leavitt's book of short stories, *Family Dancing*, uses the familiar form, language and characters but adds his own perspective, that of a gay writer in a terrifying era, to create something unfamiliar. Yet it is somehow ironic that while writers as different from each other as Joy Williams and Richard Ford have been condemned in some quarters for their uniformity, the middle-class miniaturists seem about to merge into one faint, polite and intelligent voice; it is noticeable that while this is apparently acceptable to (middle-class) critics, those who write about a different strata in American society are 'all the same'.

NOTES

1. Ann Beattie, *Where You'll Find Me* (Pavanne, 1988), p. 90.
2. Ann Beattie (ed.), *Best American Short Stories 1987* (Boston: Houghton Mifflin, 1987), p. xiv.
3. Beattie, *Where You'll Find Me*, p. 32.
4. *Granta 8: Dirty Realism* (Granta Publications, 1983), p. 5.
5. Beattie, *Where You'll Find Me*, p. 17.
6. *Granta 8: Dirty Realism*, p. 81.
7. Elizabeth Tallent, *Time with Children* (New York: Alfred A. Knopf, 1987), p. 3.
8. Duncan Webster, *Looka Yonder!* (Comedia/Routledge, 1988), p. 128.
9. Tallent, *Time with Children*, p. 110.
10. Tallent, *Time with Children*, p. 27.
11. Webster, *Looka Yonder!*, p. 130.
12. Tama Janowitz, *Slaves of New York* (Picador, 1987), p. 1.
13. Ibid., p. 8.
14. Ibid., p. 7.
15. Ibid., p. 14.
16. Ibid., p. 15.
17. Ibid., p. 231.
18. Ibid., p. 229.
19. Ibid., p. 15.
20. Ibid., p. 237.
21. Ibid., p. 244.
22. Lorrie Moore, *Self-Help* (Faber, 1985), p. 11.
23. Grace Paley, *Enormous Changes at the Last Minute* (Virago, 1979), introduction by A. S. Byatt.
24. Ibid.
25. Ibid.
26. Paley, *Enormous Changes at the Last Minute*, p. 1.
27. Moore, *Self-Help*, p. 111.

28. Paley, *Enormous Changes at the Last Minute*, introduction by A. S. Byatt.
29. Moore, *Self-Help*, p. 4.
30. Paley, *Enormous Changes at the Last Minute*, p. 161.
31. Ibid., p. 167.
32. Ibid., introduction.
33. Moore, *Self-Help*, p. 20.
34. Ibid., p. 157.
35. Ibid., p. 46.
36. Ibid., p. 46.
37. Ibid., p. 25.
38. Lorrie Moore, *Like Life* (Faber, 1990), p. 152.
39. Ibid., p. 173.
40. Ibid., p. 3.
41. Ibid., pp. 7–8.
42. Ibid., p. 16.
43. Ibid., p. 4.
44. Ibid., p. 3.
45. Ibid., p. 12.
46. Ibid., p. 12.
47. Ibid., p. 6.
48. Ibid., pp. 18–19.
49. Ibid., p. 20.
50. Ibid., p. 48.
51. Ibid., p. 67.
52. Ibid., p. 134.
53. Ibid., pp. 123–24.
54. Ibid., pp. 126–27.
55. Ibid., p. 125.
56. Ibid., p. 141.

2
Raymond Carver

Shortly before Raymond Carver's death in 1989, the American magazine *Esquire* published a diagram purporting to show the current state of play in American publishing. The diagram was in the form of interconnected circles; the circle furthest away from the centre circle, the 'red-hot centre of the publishing universe', contained the least influential name. Raymond Carver appeared in the centre circle.

In the few years before he died, Carver's influence was quite extraordinary. In a 1987 interview, David Applefield points out to Carver that 'Some literary editors claim that nearly half of the short fiction they receive seems imitative of your style.' In Mark Helprin's shrill introduction to *The Best American Short Stories 1988* he complains that

> Of the stories read for the purpose of gathering the twenty herein, more than a third dealt with divorce, separation or extramarital affairs. Alcohol appeared in more than half, cigarettes and coffee in more than a third, brand names in about a third, and that satanic square that I can hardly bear to mention, television, in more than half.[1]

It is not hard to recognize the influence of the 'Dirty Realists' in general, and Carver in particular, from this paragraph (it is perhaps worth noting that Helprin's final selection for the anthology, made 'blind', included stories by Carver, Tobias Wolff and Louise Erdich).

Elsewhere Helprin lambasts the 'minimalist' school ('Why are so many minimalist stories about despicable people in filthy unkempt garden apartments filled with ugly bric-à-brac, where everyone smokes, drinks, stays up all night and is addicted to coffee?') and again, Carver would appear to be central to the editor's preoccupations.

'Minimalism' is a term that writers such as Carver and Bobbie Ann Mason have fended off wearily for some time now. 'Someone, meaning it as praise, called me a "Minimalist", and I didn't like that, it just made me feel uncomfortable', Carver told David Sexton in 1985. 'There are great minimalist painters, writers and composers, I guess, but it made me uncomfortable. I thought, maybe I've taken out too much.'[2] Mason used a very similar line in her interview with the author of this book in 1989:

> In the States, the only time I get associated with those other authors (Carver, Wolff, Ford *et al.*) is when critics start throwing around the term 'minimalism', which I dislike because it's derogatory. It implies that there's not much substance.[3]

According to Carver, his own 'minimalism' was brought about by the circumstances he found himself in when he was a struggling writer. These circumstances were, by anyone's definition, spectacularly desperate: when Carver married at 18, his wife was 16 and already pregnant, and a second child followed shortly afterwards. In 'Fires', perhaps the most sensible essay on a writer's influences ever published, Carver describes this period of his life:

> In those days I always worked some crap job or another, and my wife did the same. She waitressed or else was a door-to-door saleswoman. Years later she taught high school. But that was years later. I worked sawmill jobs, janitor jobs, delivery man jobs, service station jobs, stockroom boy jobs—name it, I did it. One summer, in Arcata, California, I picked tulips, I swear, during the daylight hours, to support us; and at night, after closing, I cleaned the inside of a drive-in restaurant and swept up the parking lot.[4]

Attempting a novel was unthinkable at this time: 'So I purposely, and by necessity, limited myself to writing things I could finish in one sitting, two sittings at the most.' Elsewhere in the essay Carver describes in moving detail the frustration he felt one Saturday afternoon in a laundromat (Saturday being a day on which he hoped to be able to write) when a woman restarted a dryer that he was hoping to use:

> . . . I remember thinking at that moment . . . that nothing—and brother, I mean nothing—that ever happened to me on this earth could come anywhere close, could possibly be as important to me, could make as much difference, as the fact that I had two children. And that I would always have them and always find myself in this position of unrelieved responsibility and permanent distraction. . . . I'm talking about real *influence* now. I'm talking about the moon and the tide.[5]

This puts a lot of the writing about Carver—his minimalism, his debts to Hemingway and Chekhov—into perspective. Carver wrote short stories (and poetry) because initially he was unable to write anything else, and later because it was a form with which he felt entirely comfortable. It is a form that still provokes prejudice in some critics: in an obituary of Carver in the *Guardian*, W. J. Weatherby argued that

> . . . his first novel was to decide how important a writer he might be. Could he carry over into a long narrative his evocation of the life of the American white working class that succeeded so well in his short stories? But he left the answer unfinished.[6]

Why the novel should remain the only medium that can admit greatness remains something of a mystery; elsewhere Weatherby's obituary argues that 'some of [Carver's] own work could stand the comparison' with Chekhov; elsewhere a posthumous review of his last collection in the *Sunday Times* was entitled, simply, 'The American Chekhov'.[7] They are accolades that belong to a major literary figure, not to someone whose potential remained unfulfilled.

The rest of Carver's story has been exhaustively documented in reviews and interviews. These years of extreme poverty ('There was a period of ten years when we were horribly poor, we were the working poor'[8]) ended with the marriage broken and Carver wrecked by alcoholism. On 2 June 1977, what he came to refer to as his 'second life' began: he quit drinking, a year or so after the publication of his first collection of stories,

Raymond Carver

Will You Please Be Quiet, Please, met his second wife, the poet Tess Gallagher, and achieved a decade of phenomenal success and apparently deep happiness before his death from lung cancer in 1988. During that decade he published three more collections of stories: *What We Talk About When We Talk About Love*, *Cathedral* and *Elephant* (published in the U.S. as *Where I'm Calling From*), as well as numerous collections of poetry.

It is significant, I think, that whereas in the U.S. Carver's work has been described as 'minimalist', in the U.K. he is regarded as the Godfather of 'Dirty Realism'. Neither term, in truth, actually means very much at all, but they reveal a great deal both about the attitudes of the respective countries towards this sort of writing, and about the state of each country's contemporary literature.

When *Granta*'s *Dirty Realism* anthology first appeared, in 1983, English fiction still consisted for the most part of a small but dominant group of writers—Drabble, Murdoch, the two Amises, Lodge, Bradbury, etc.—whose work came to define the predominant strain in the contemporary novel. These novelists were resolutely middle-class (most of their novels were set either in universities or in the leafy streets of comfortable London suburbs) and though individually they are all possessed of enormous strengths, collectively they had begun to take on a depressingly moribund aspect.

It is thus hardly surprising that whereas in the States critics responded to the *style* of the work of Carver, Ford, Mason *et al.*, in the U.K. it was the *content* of their stories that attracted attention. British reviewers had read very little like this for twenty-five years, when Barstow and Braine and Sillitoe were first published. The exiled American editor of *Granta*, Bill Buford, cleverly exploited the lack of an alternative viewpoint in Britain when he invented the term 'Dirty Realism' specially for the anthology; he understood that whereas no great interest was likely to be created by the term 'minimalism', a punchy new movement which apparently drew attention to America's under-belly would prove irresistible to readers heartily sick of delicate delineations of

Hampstead life. Buford described his collection as

> ... unadorned, unfurnished, low-rent tragedies about people who watch day-time television, read cheap romances or listen to country and western music. They are waitresses in roadside cafes, cashiers in supermarkets, construction workers, secretaries and unemployed cowboys. They play bingo, eat cheeseburgers, hunt deer and stay in cheap hotels. They drink a lot and are often in trouble: for stealing a car, breaking a window, pick-pocketing a wallet. They are from Kentucky or Alabama or Oregon, but, mainly, they could just about be from anywhere: drifters in a world cluttered with junk food and the oppressive details of modern consumerism.[9]

They eat cheeseburgers! Seven years on, Buford's introduction reads as though it was written for Bertie Wooster and Lord Peter Wimsey, but it was effective in creating interest. However, it also helped to create an image that Carver was never really able to shake off in this country, as some kind of spokesman for the mid-west poor. W. J. Weatherby's obituary observed that 'Typical Carver characters are American couples whose dreams have ended in their struggle to pay the rent and who keep going, patching up their lives and their marriages.' Picador's collection of the first three volumes of Carver's stories includes a quotation from *Vogue* comparing Carver to Edward Hopper; even in 1989, just after Carver's death, a B.B.C. *Omnibus* documentary begins with scenes filmed in a suitably unpretentious diner. In Reagan's '80s, this version of the U.S. was the most fashionable in the U.K.; those figures alienated from the American mainstream, the James Deans and the Marlowes and the Hopper characters, were the only Americans that the young British intelligentsia were allowed to like. In the *New York Times*, however, Christopher Lehmann-Haupt could review Carver's final volume of stories without once having to refer to the class of the characters depicted in it.[10]

My argument is not that British responses to Carver's work predictably concentrate on class where none is implied: that is obviously not the case. 'Night School', from *Will You Please Be Quiet, Please*, begins: 'My marriage had just fallen apart. I couldn't find a job. I had another girl. But she wasn't in town. So I was at a bar having a glass of beer. . .'[11]; the two women he meets in the bar are learning to read at night school. The first two lines of the very next story, 'Collectors', are: 'I was out of work. But any day I expected to hear from up north.'[12]

But both these stories develop in a way that would possibly surprise readers previously only familiar with Carver's work through second-hand accounts. It is certainly not Carver's intention to bring the working poor to the notice of the American public, Steinbeck-style; 'Night School' is a portrait of a man without emotional or financial support, but Carver's approach is muted, oblique, almost perplexed. 'Collectors' covers similar territory, but is an account of a collision between two desperate men, one waiting to hear news about a job, the other a door-to-door vacuum salesman approaching the verge of insanity. The details of poverty and social ignominy are not glossed over: in 'Night School', the narrator must wait for the women to offer him a drink, and goes to the café where his mother waitresses for a free supper. But they are Carver's materials, not the finished product, and to concentrate on them is to miss the point of the stories. These are miniaturized observations of how we behave under extreme circumstances, and not portraits of the circumstances themselves.

In any case, too much has been made of Carver's social realism, at the expense of his acute perceptions of human sensibilities. There are several stories in Carver's first collection in which references to money or its absence are conspicuously missing. 'Bicycles, muscles, cigarets', for example, possibly the strongest story in *Will You Please Be Quiet, Please*, features a model mid-western family, a family which is not, as far as we are aware, facing the prospect of bankruptcy or separation.

'Bicycles, muscles, cigarets' is not atypical of Carver's work, and punctures several myths about both 'minimalism' and 'Dirty Realism'. Mark Helprin, in his infamous introduction, remarked that the minimalists

> . . . observe everything of great moment as if from a great distance, as if it were in miniature, or under glass, as if when you pricked them, they would not bleed. Whence comes their

gluttonous pursuit of irony, their unlikely detachment in regard to love and death?[13]

In 'Bicycles . . .' Carver's approach may not be straightforward, but it is not detached. The central character of the story, Evan Hamilton, is trying desperately to give up smoking; on the second evening of his attempt he is summoned by a boy he has never met to a neighbouring house, where his son Roger is being questioned by an irate mother. The mother wants to know the part that Roger and two other boys, Kip and Gary Berman, played in the disappearance of her son's bicycle.

Hamilton, still distracted by his craving, expresses proper and balanced disapproval of Roger's minor vandalism, but when Gary Berman's father, a bull-headed man only prepared to listen to his mendacious son, arrives on the scene, he swiftly provokes Evan into a fight, and the two men end up rolling around on their neighbours' lawn.

It is an extraordinarily detailed story, less than eight pages long, and an object lesson in brilliantly realized complexity for anyone who wishes to write fiction. The point here, however, is that Carver uses the set-up to discuss nothing less than the inevitable separation of father and son through death; there is none of the detachment that Helprin refers to.

The fight reminds Hamilton of his own father ('Hamilton had loved his father and could recall many things about him. But now he recalled his father's one fistfight as if it were all there was to the man'[14]); later, when Roger has gone to bed, coincidentally he too begins to remember his grandfather, and wants to understand the relationship between Evan and his father when Evan was his own age. Evan's strength in the fight has made Roger aware of his father's mortality:

> Dad? You'll think I'm pretty crazy, but I wish I'd known you when you were little. I mean, about as old as I am right now. I don't know how to say it, but I'm lonesome about it. It's like . . . it's like I miss you already if I think about it now. That's pretty crazy, isn't it?[15]

This is the side of Carver's work that has been overlooked in attempts to create a figure-head for one or other of the two literary movements associated with him. There are other stories in his first book which similarly contradict narrower definitions of his concerns: the title story in the collection is a powerful examination of an otherwise mundane schoolteacher's brief descent into madness when he realizes that his wife was unfaithful to him some years previously; and 'How about this?' is an account of a couple's doomed attempt to move from the city to the country.

In *What We Talk About When We Talk About Love*, a new dimension is introduced into his work. In a sense it is Carver at his most Carveresque; the ellipsis that he had already appeared to be groping for in the earlier book becomes even more marked. ('Everything I thought I could live without, I just got rid of', he told David Sexton in reference to the second collection. 'It felt like I'd gone as far in that direction as I wished to go.'[16])

A number of first lines show a sophistication to the blank realism of the beginnings in the first collection, so that the reader is launched into a series of blackly comic and bizarre episodes without time to orient him- or herself. 'A man without hands came to the door to sell me a photograph of my house' ('Viewfinder'[17]). 'That morning she pours Teacher's over my belly and licks it off. That afternoon she tries to jump out of the window' ('Gazebo'[18]). 'I'll tell you what did my father in. The third thing was Dummy, that Dummy died' ('The third thing that killed my father off'[19]). 'In the kitchen, he poured himself another drink and looked at the bedroom suite in his front yard' ('Why don't you dance?'[20]).

In the interview with David Sexton quoted above, Carver remarked that at this stage in his career, he felt that he would 'soon be writing stories I wouldn't want to read myself', and as a consequence did not write anything until several months after the completion of *What We Talk About When We Talk About Love*. One irony of this book is that because of the extreme spareness of the writing, some of the stories resemble the kind of experimentalism against which Carver's work is usually held in contrast. Several of the stories are little more than three pages long; and in some places the short lines of elliptical dialogue, together with their author's occasional

antipathy to speech marks, are reminiscent of Pinter:
> Hey, the boy said.
> I'm sorry, the girl said.
> It's all right, the boy said.
> I didn't mean to snap like that.
> It was my fault, he said.
> You sit down. How does a waffle sound with bacon.[21]

If there is experimentation here, it is of a quasi-meta-fictional nature; Carver seems to be pushing at the limits of realism by gutting nearly everything we have come to accept as constituting fiction. In the story quoted, 'Everything stuck to him', there is little sense of time or place (the first sentence, 'She's in Milan for Christmas', is left undeveloped in any literal way), and the short sentences actually begin to become intrusive, whereas their original intention was presumably to draw attention away from the text and towards the world of the characters. There inevitably comes a point at which unstylized prose of this order starts to become self-conscious, almost self-referential.

It is interesting, therefore, that Carver chose to rewrite several of the stories from his second collection. Some of them appear in *Fires*, retitled, and another, 'The bath', appears in *Cathedral* as 'A small, good thing', regarded in some quarters as Carver's masterpiece; an examination of the changes that the author made is instructive and revealing.

'Everything stuck to him', retitled 'Distance' in *Fires*, undergoes only slight alterations, but they are indicative of the dissatisfactions that Carver obviously felt with this particular stage of his work. Several times Carver joins together sentences in the rewritten version: thus, 'The boy loved to hunt, you see. That's part of it' becomes one sentence in 'Distance', suggesting that Carver was unhappy with the rhythm of his prose. And there are a number of additional details in 'Distance' which add flesh to the skeletal framework of the original: brief descriptions of the boy's friend Carl, and slight elaborations to the Milanese setting, serve to make the author's approach something slightly more conventional.

Interestingly, the only change to the narrative results in 'Distance' becoming slightly more emotionally engaged than 'Everything stuck to him'; in the first story, it is as if Carver over-compensates for the potentially sentimental nature of his material (young father changes his mind about leaving his wife and sick baby behind while he goes on a hunting trip). In 'Distance', Carver includes a scene where 'the boy' explains to Carl why he cannot after all hunt with him, an explanation accepted calmly by the older man:

> It's cleared up, Carl said. I don't look for much action this morning. Probably you won't have missed anything anyway.
> The boy nodded. I'll see you, Carl, he said.
> So long, Carl said. Hey, don't let anyone tell you otherwise, Carl said. You're a lucky boy and I mean that.[22]

One could scarcely accuse Carver of gross over-indulgence here; the writing is as understated as ever. And in any case, the author has already created a complicated flashback structure which prohibits a banal interpretation of the story. The episode is recounted by an older man to his adult daughter, and the implication is that he is the boy and she the sick baby. The fact that they are alone, and that they are in Milan (the 'Distance' of the title is emotional and physical) suggests that the marriage has been dissolved. Thus a narrative that in the hands of a lesser writer could have been an uninteresting rites-of-passage cliché (boy discovers that family is more important than immature male pursuits) becomes a clever and quietly moving deconstruction of an apparently significant moment. Carver does not rewrite the final paragraph of 'Everything stuck to him'; the man instructs his daughter to get ready for a guided tour of Milan while he recalls his return from Carl's house:

> They had laughed. They had leaned on each other and laughed until the tears had come, while everything else—the cold, and where he'd go in it—was outside, for a while, anyway.[23]

The reader understands that the reunion was only of ephemeral importance, and therein lies the story's emotional punch. 'Distance' is a quietly devastating complexification of memory, and Carver's rewrite gives it room to breathe.

'Mr. Coffee and Mr. Fixit' from the second collection undergoes a much more radical modification in *Fires*, in which it appears as 'Where is everyone?'. The original story is Carver at his most elliptical: one of his disaffected male characters draws a bewildering picture of his relationships with his unfaithful wife and her lover, his promiscuous mother and the death of his father. The story is less than three pages long.

This, perhaps, is the kind of approach that Carver had in mind when he said that he would soon be writing stories that he would not want to read himself. It is not a story that can sustain repeated reading, not because of its brevity—'I could see the smallest things', from the same collection, is no longer, but works because it isolates a moment—but because it uses its ellipsis for comic effect. 'Where is everyone?' is still very funny (David Sexton quotes a reviewer saying 'I laughed all the way through the story—but it was awkward, uneasy laughter'), but the humour derives from its substance rather than its absences:

> A lot has happened since that afternoon, and on the whole things are better now. But during those days, when my mother was putting out to men she'd just met, I was out of work, drinking and crazy. My kids were crazy, and my wife was crazy and having a 'thing' with an unemployed aerospace engineer she'd met at AA. He was crazy too. His name was Ross and he had five or six kids. He walked with a limp from a gunshot wound his first wife had given him. He didn't have a wife now; he wanted my wife. I don't know what we were all thinking of in those days.[24]

There is an equivalent passage in the first story, but the rewritten version is better because its greater length allows Carver to represent the gloomy circularity of the narrator's plight in the repetitions of the prose.

'Mr. Coffee and Mr. Fixit' seems closer to the spirit of Beckett's work than it does to, say, Hemingway's; there is a similar sense that what is articulated is actually of little consequence, and certainly an inadequate response to the situation. There are several other stories in this vein: 'Gazebo' and 'Viewfinder' in particular convey a similar sense of the absurd. But it is in the transformation of 'The bath' into 'A small, good thing' that we can see most clearly what Carver wanted to move away from and towards.

'The bath' is a typically skeletal account of a road accident involving a young boy, Scotty, and its effect on his parents. There is an undercurrent of menace in the story, which derives from a series of apparently menacing 'phone calls that the parents receive: in fact, they are from a baker demanding payment for a cake (the accident occurs on the boy's birthday) that the parents have forgotten to pick up, and Carver ends the tale with such a call:

> The telephone rang.
> 'Yes!' she said. 'Hello!' she said.
> 'Mrs. Weiss,' a man's voice said.
> 'Yes,' she said. 'This is Mrs. Weiss. Is it about Scotty?' she said.
> 'Scotty,' the voice said. 'It is about Scotty,' the voice said. 'It has to do with Scotty, yes.'[25]

'The bath' is a moderately effective conglomeration of inappropriacies and ironies, given greater resonance by the apparently harmless nature of the accident (Scotty walks back from school apparently unconcerned, but lapses into a coma while telling his mother about his experience), and Carver provides no resolution; the boy is left in his coma, and the parents never discover the source of the 'phone calls. It is not, however, the most memorable of the stories in the second collection, and its metamorphosis as 'A small, good thing' shows how Carver under-exploited his material in the middle stage of his career.

In 'A small, good thing', Carver carries forward the situation left unresolved in the original story. Scotty, the son, dies in hospital; on their return home the parents are again harassed by 'phone calls from the baker, who still does not reveal his identity, and the mother finally remembers the cake. She asks her husband to drive her to the shopping mall so that she can confront him, but instead of confrontation, the couple find themselves eating the baker's bread ('Eating is a small, good thing at a time like this', he tells them[26]) and listening to him talk about his life:

> They listened carefully. Although they were tired and in anguish, they listened to what the baker had to say. They nodded when the baker began to speak of loneliness, and of

the sense of doubt and limitation that had come to him in his middle years. He told them what it was like to be childless all these years. . . . They talked on into the early morning, the high, pale cast of light in the windows, and they did not think of leaving.[27]

There are a number of points that arise from this extraordinary story. One is struck by how Carver's unadorned prose style is an ideal medium for an emotive subject such as that covered here; the author's refusal to manipulate the reader allows a more complex response, and paradoxically his apparently disengaged approach focuses the story's power. It is worth noting, incidentally, that the strongest works by three of the writers discussed in this volume—Anne Tyler's *The Accidental Tourist*, Richard Ford's *The Sportswriter* and 'A small, good thing'—all centre around the death of a child (and were all written within four years of each other). It is interesting to compare Frank Bascombe's account of his son's death in *The Sportswriter* with Carver's story:

> We were both sitting beside his bed. It was early in the morning. Before light. We may have been asleep, really. But a nurse came in and said, 'I'm sorry, Mr. Bascombe. Ralph has expired.' We both sat there a few minutes, stunned, though we knew it was going to happen. And then she cried a while and I did, too. And then I went home and cooked up some bacon and toast, and ended up watching television.[28]

'I think you want to eat when someone dies'[29] girl-friend Vicki tells Bascombe a little later; it is perhaps unsurprising that Carver and Ford, the two great literalists, should have their characters respond more or less identically to death.

'A small, good thing' marks a progression from the unresolved, oblique, surreally stripped-down stories in *What We Talk About When We Talk About Love*, particularly in the tenderness of its ending. Carver recognized the change in tone; 'I think that in the book *Cathedral* a lot of the stories are fuller and more interesting, for me anyway, than any of the other stories', he said in 1985.

The story 'Fever', for instance—where the wife has gone away and left him with the kids. 'A small, good thing', that's a story where people make connection after the baby has died. But my life has changed and I think it's fair to say I'm becoming more optimistic.[30]

Stories dealing with the death of a child or a painful separation may not sound like the product of an increased optimism. But given Carver's previous predilection for leaving his characters in a state of spiritual terror at the end of a story (and 'The bath' is a fine example of how he used a lack of resolution to recreate a state of despair), this new faith in the human spirit's ability to adapt and endure does represent a movement away from hopelessness.

In 'Fever', the dilemma of Carlyle, the central character, is superficially banal—he cannot find a suitable baby-sitter for his children—and yet it recalls Carver's comments on children and influence in the essay 'Fires'. Carlyle's new relationship with a secretary from the school where he teaches, his job, his lingering love for his departed wife, all these factors are insignificant compared to the fact that he cannot provide adequate provision or care for his son and daughter while he is at work. Salvation eventually comes in the form of an elderly lady whose goodness and competence serve to lift Carlyle's burden from him; when she announces that she has to leave his employ because her husband is taking work out of the area, Carlyle uses the occasion (and the distortion brought on by the eponymous sickness) to describe to Mrs. Webster how he came to find himself in his current state.

Effectively 'Fever' is a reprise of 'A small, good thing': just as the parents in the latter story are apparently left rearmed, readjusted by their conversation with the baker, Carlyle's 'connection' with Mrs. Webster leaves him able to reappraise his own recent history when he waves goodbye to the baby-sitter:

> It was then, as he stood at the window, that he felt something come to an end. It had to do with Eileen and the life before this. Had he ever waved at her? He must have, of course, he knew he had, yet he could not remember just now. But he understood it was over, and he felt able to let her go. He was sure their life together had happened in the way he

said it had. But it was something that had passed. And that passing—though it had seemed impossible and he'd fought against it—would become a part of him now, too, as surely as anything else he'd left behind.[31]

Both prose—still plain, but more generous, less clipped—and sentiment here are typical of the Carver to be found in this third volume of stories; and Carlyle's internal momentum is another innovation in the author's work.

The title story, the last one in the volume, is another in which the narrator makes discernible progress towards some kind of conclusive discovery, and as in 'Fever' and 'A small, good thing' the story ends with an unexpected connection. The slightly bizarre subject-matter and the dead-beat no-hoper narrator are reminiscent of the material in the first two collections: 'Cathedral' is an account of the narrator's relationship with a blind man, an old friend of his wife, who comes to stay. Like so much of Carver's work, it is a story about communication, about how people with no common language can communicate effectively. In 'Cathedral' it is not the visitor's blindness that inhibits contact between the two men (although as far as the narrator is aware this is exactly the problem); rather, it is the narrator's dependence on well-worn cultural paths (television, crass small-talk) which inevitably exclude his guest. In the end a nexus is formed, but only when all attempts at verbal intercourse have ceased. The narrator is attempting to describe a cathedral he is watching on television, but his attempts are entirely inadequate, and at the exhilarating conclusion of the story, the blind man holds onto the pen while his host draws the building: 'I put in windows with arches. I drew flying buttresses. I hung great doors. I couldn't stop.'[32] This new medium liberates the narrator; when the blind man asks him to close his eyes and feel the drawing, he finds that he does not want to open them again: 'I was in my house. I knew that. But I didn't feel I was inside anything.'[33]

At the end of 1988, a few months after Carver's death, a memorial evening was held for him in a London night-club on a wet Sunday evening. Tess Gallagher, Carver's widow, was there, of course, and read one of her late husband's poems; Richard Ford and Joy Williams each read a story, as did Salman Rushdie, in one of his last public appearances before the publication of *The Satanic Verses*. The guest of honour was a distinguished-looking elderly gentleman referred to as 'Sir Victor'—V. S. Pritchett, the English story-writer and essayist.

When critics place Carver in a literary tradition, it is always an exclusively American one: his work invariably reminds them of Cheever, Hemingway, Welty and so on. After the publication of *Elephant*, Carver's final collection (whose seven stories appeared in the U.S. alongside a retrospective of earlier work in an anthology entitled *Where I'm Calling From*), the story 'Errand', which deals somewhat uncharacteristically with the last hours of Chekhov's life, provoked several comparisons with the Russian writer—more or less the only European name to appear in reviews of Carver's work.

Yet in an interview with Pritchett in the *Guardian* in 1990, James Wood observed that

> Some of Pritchett's early fictional dialogue, with its obsessive syntax and its attention to the stiff colloquial mechanics of intercourse, seems unremarkable enough today, but only if one forgets that Pritchett came before Pinter.

Wood goes on to quote Pritchett as saying 'Sometimes ordinary speech is banal, and it is always repetitive, but if selected with art it can reveal the inner life, often fantastic, in the speaker.'[34]

Perhaps it is no surprise, then, that Pritchett and Carver seemed to have formed a bond (and it is salutary to observe how writers make connections where critics have found none); certainly Carver would have strongly appreciated Pritchett's observation. It is not true to say that all of Carver's writing reveals a similar fascination for the banalities of everyday speech; frequently he allows his characters to be piercingly articulate about their lives. At the end of 'The student's wife', for example, in which a sleepless night provokes a near-nervous breakdown in the eponymous woman, the end of the story has her down on her knees saying 'God . . . God, will you help us, God?'[35]; one of the myths about Carver's work is that nearly all of the created tensions are formed by the gap between the situation the characters find themselves in and their ability to verbalize it.

Elephant is interesting because the marked progression visible in *Cathedral* is continued, and yet in two or three of the stories Carver seems to be returning to examinations of the nexus between articulacy and appropriacy that he touched on earlier in his career. 'Fate sent her to die on the couch in our living room in Germany', says Mrs. Morgan to Myers in 'Put yourself in my shoes' (from *Will You Please Be Quiet, Please*, a title which in itself hints at the linguistic concerns found in the collection); usually this kind of infelicitous expression would be presented to us without comment, but Myers is a writer:

> Myers began to laugh. 'Fate . . . sent . . . her . . . to . . . die . . . in . . . your . . . living . . . room?' he said between gasps.
> 'Is that funny, sir?' Morgan said. 'Do you find that amusing?'
> Myers nodded. He kept laughing. He wiped his eye on his shirt sleeve. 'I'm really sorry,' he said. 'I can't help it. That line. . . .'[36]

This is perhaps the crudest manifestation of Carver's obsession with the banality of his characters' vernacular (and there is a surprising and atypical degree of cruelty evident in this passage); in *Elephant* his use of everyday speech has become extraordinarily sophisticated.

'Intimacy', from the last collection, provides a useful comparison with 'Put yourself in my shoes' because it also features a writer, the first-person narrator of the story. The narrator pays a visit to his first wife; it is their first meeting for four years, and within minutes she launches a savage, withering assault on him, in the face of which he is almost mute:

> As soon as I sit down she brings me some coffee. Then she comes out with what's on her mind. She says I've caused her anguish, made her feel exposed and humiliated. Make no mistake, I feel I'm home.[37]

The cause of this anger would appear to be the writer's use of his past life as material for his fiction: 'What's done is done and water under the bridge, she says. A tragedy, yes. God knows it was a tragedy and then some. But why keep it going?'[38] The story makes frequent use of similar commonplaces and clichés ('I think you're crazy as a bedbug',[39] 'What the hell do you want from me? Blood?',[40] 'Your heart is a jungle, a dark forest, it's a garbage pail, if you want to know'[41]); and occasionally the wife's attempts to articulate her rage and disgust result in phrases containing a peculiar, blackly comic juxtaposition of *aperçu* and exhausted vernacular ('We were so intimate I could puke'[42]) or in sentiments whose poison manages to transcend the impotence of their expression: 'I think if you were on fire right now, if you suddenly burst into flame this minute, I wouldn't throw a bucket of water on you'[43]; 'Honey, no offence, but sometimes I think I could shoot you and watch you kick.'[44] The incongruity of the 'no offence' in the latter quotation is important: in 'Intimacy' language is a gun which fires both blanks and live bullets indiscriminately.

'Intimacy' contains an impressive number of ideas in its eight pages. Ostensibly it deals with the responsibility of the writer (who has no answer to the vicious charges, and can only respond by getting on his knees and clutching at the hem of his former wife's dress) and his predilection for the cannibalization of his own past. ('You know why you're here. You're on a fishing expedition. You're hunting for material',[45] the woman accuses him. The final irony of the story, of course, is that the charge is proven.) Ultimately, however, it is about words, their inadequacy and their power; when the narrator takes his leave of this woman and sees 'this white moon hanging in the morning sky', he is 'afraid to comment on it. I am. I don't know what might happen. I might break into tears even. I might not understand a word I'd say.'[45] 'Intimacy' is the writer's inevitably doomed attempt to shut up and listen.

'Blackbird Pie', the penultimate story in the volume, shows similar interests in words and language. Here the narrator's wife pushes a letter under his study door informing him of her intention to move out; again, there is a sense in the letter of a floundering to find the phrase that will hit home:

Dear,
Things are not good. Things, in fact, are bad. Things have gone from bad to worse. And you know what I'm talking

about.... The time has come, you see, to admit that *the impossible* has happened. To cry *Uncle*. To beg off. To—⁴⁶

For the narrator, this communication is complicated by the fact that he is convinced that the handwriting is not his wife's, a conviction never explained in the narrative, but which serves to add a surreality further adduced by the appearance of two horses from out of the fog as the wife is about to leave. The mysterious handwriting seems to be a way of divorcing language from its source: if the handwriting is unfamiliar, then the contents of the letter become random, unconnected, almost meaningless, and the narrator ends up by extracting odd phrases 'which might under different circumstances serve as a kind of abstract':

> ... withdrawing farther into ... a small enough thing, but ... talcum powder sprayed over the bathroom, including walls and baseboards ... a shell ... not to mention the insane asylum ... until finally ... a balanced view .... the grave. ...⁴⁷

And so on. At the story's conclusion, the narrator makes an observation which is uncharacteristic for a Carver character in its abstracted perception and its direct articulation:

> It could be said ... that to take a wife is to take a history. And if that's so, then I understand that I'm outside history now—like horses and fog. Or you could say my history has left me. Or that I'm having to go on without history.... That's when it dawns on me that autobiography is the poor man's history. And that I am saying goodbye to history. Goodbye my darling.⁴⁸

In a tiny story entitled 'The Father' (in *Will You Please Be Quiet, Please*) Carver touches on a similar idea: a family group discusses a baby's family resemblances, and conclude that 'Daddy doesn't look like *anybody*!'; when they turn to look at the father, 'his face was white and without expression.'⁴⁹ Like the narrator in 'Blackbird Pie', his history has abandoned him. It is somehow apt that in the penultimate story of Carver's last collection (and as the last story is 'Errand', the final story to deal with these modern American characters) the author should finally disclose the extra dimension that these separations and divorces and lonelinesses have always had.

I would not wish to suggest that the seven stories in *Elephant* are somehow experimental, or that Carver is so busy examining the nature of language that he has abandoned his old concerns. The title story corresponds almost exactly to the idea of Carver as social realist propagated by the likes of W. J. Weatherby; it depicts the plight of a man burdened with the crippling financial support of his mother, his brother, his son, his daughter and his former wife:

> Once in a while I'd get fed up with it and write letters to all of them, threatening to change my name and telling them I was going to quit my job. I'd tell them I was planning a move to Australia. And the thing was, I was serious when I'd say that about Australia, even though I didn't know the first thing about Australia. I just knew that it was on the other side of the world, and that's where I wanted to be.[50]

It is an intolerable situation, but also one that he cannot change. He knows that these fantasies of Australia are simply fantasies, and in any case his continued bankrolling of a group of adults who should be able to pay their own way seems to be some form of expiation for his earlier alcoholism. There is no way out for him, but the human spirit finds ways to escape anyway. The narrator dreams that he is riding on his father's back, pretending that he is an elephant; the temporary freedom provokes a sweet burst of optimism and acceptance:

> When all was said and done, things could be a lot worse. People's luck had gone south on them was all. Things would pick up in the fall maybe. There was lots to hope for.[51]

The story ends with the narrator speeding along in his colleague's 'big, unpaid-for car'; as in 'Cathedral', a vision of freedom does not necessarily have to be accompanied by a change in circumstance.

It is impossible to discuss the last story in *Elephant* without referring to its eerie prescience: 'Errand' is a portrait of a great writer dying slowly of a lung disease, a portrait created by an artist of similar stature suffering the same fate. It is the only Carver story to be set outside the U.S., and the only one set in a specific past, as opposed to an indistinct present: these features have led some critics into describing it as entirely uncharacteristic of his work, and yet these ostensibly alien surfaces are misleading. Robert Winder has perceptively drawn parallels between Carver's description of the death of Chekhov ('Then Chekhov turned on his side. He closed his eyes and sighed. A minute later his breathing stopped.') and the similarly 'perfunctory' death of Scotty in 'A small, good thing' ('His lips parted as his last breath was puffed through his throat and exhaled gently through the clenched teeth'[52]). Winder points out that 'All the emotions are buried in the remarkable fact of the champagne.'[53] (The doctor treating Chekhov, knowing that the end is near, has ordered a bottle to be brought to the writer's room: 'It was one of those rare moments of inspiration that can easily enough be overlooked later on, because the action is so entirely appropriate it seems inevitable.'[54]) Like the baker's bread, the champagne is a small, good thing.

There are other tiny physical details that Carver homes in on in 'Errand': the story closes with a bell-boy reaching down to rescue the cork from the champagne bottle, his discomfiture at being in the presence of the great man's corpse searching desperately for an outlet. This is not symbolism; rather, it is an acute observation of how the most articulate and potent revelations are to be found in gesture rather than in speech. The beautiful understatement of the last line here seems an entirely fitting conclusion to the career of a writer who managed to capture life's most transcendent moments by concentrating on their details.

The scope of this essay does not extend far enough to encompass Carver's poetry; yet in the posthumous collection *A New Path to the Waterfall* there are so many lines that one would wish to quote, not to illuminate Carver's prose work necessarily (although many of the poems certainly do shed light on the stories, and Tess Gallagher's introduction is essential reading for any serious Carver student), but to illustrate the writer's humbling generosity of spirit, his bravery—many of the poems were composed in the full knowledge that he had very little time left to write—and his honesty. In 'Gravy' he provides a crushing summation of his post-alcoholic career:

> Eleven years
> ago he was told he had six months to live
> at the rate he was going. And he was going
> nowhere but down. So he changed his ways
> somehow. He quit drinking! And the rest?
> After that it was *all* gravy, every minute
> of it, up to and including when he was told about,
> well, some things that were breaking down and
> building up inside his head. 'Don't weep for me,'
> he said to his friends. 'I'm a lucky man.
> I've had ten years longer than I or anyone
> expected. Pure gravy. And don't forget it.'[55]

His friends, those young writers whose cause he championed tirelessly and those who loved his work will find it hard to accept these sentiments now, but their warmth and clarity serve as an eloquent valediction.

NOTES

1. Mark Helprin (ed.), *Best American Short Stories 1988* (Boston: Houghton Mifflin, 1988), p. xxiii.
2. *Literary Review*, July 1985.
3. *Sunday Telegraph*, 12 December 1989.
4. Raymond Carver, *Fires* (Picador, 1986), p. 34.
5. Ibid., p. 33.
6. *Guardian*, 5 August 1988.
7. *Sunday Times*, 6 August 1988.
8. *Literary Review*, July 1985.
9. *Granta 8: Dirty Realism*, 1983, p. 4.
10. *New York Times*, 11 May 1988.
11. Raymond Carver, *The Stories of Raymond Carver* (Picador, 1985), p. 76.
12. Ibid., p. 81.
13. Mark Helprin (ed.), *Best American Short Stories 1988* (Boston: Houghton Mifflin, 1988), pp. xxi–xxii.
14. Carver, p. 149.
15. Ibid., p. 151.
16. *Literary Review*, July 1985.
17. Carver, p. 192.

18. Ibid., p. 198.
19. Ibid., p. 241.
20. Ibid., p. 187.
21. Ibid., p. 268.
22. Raymond Carver, *Fires*, p. 136.
23. Ibid., p. 139.
24. Ibid., p. 173.
25. Raymond Carver, *The Stories of Raymond Carver*, p. 220.
26. Ibid., p. 351.
27. Ibid., p. 351.
28. Richard Ford, *The Sportswriter* (Collins Harvill, 1986), p. 66.
29. Ibid., p. 67.
30. *Literary Review*, July 1985.
31. Carver, p. 417.
32. Ibid., p. 446.
33. Ibid., p. 447.
34. *Guardian*, 8 February 1990.
35. Carver, p. 100.
36. Ibid., p. 111.
37. Carver, *Elephant* (Collins Harvill, 1988), p. 45.
38. Ibid., p. 46.
39. Ibid., p. 46.
40. Ibid., p. 46.
41. Ibid., p. 49.
42. Ibid., p. 47.
43. Ibid., p. 49.
44. Ibid., p. 50.
45. Ibid., pp. 47–8.
46. Ibid., p. 93.
47. Ibid., p. 100.
48. Ibid., p. 109.
49. *The Stories of Raymond Carver*, p. 41.
50. Carver, *Elephant*, p. 80.
51. Ibid., p. 88.
52. *The Stories of Raymond Carver*, p. 345.
53. *Independent*, 11 August 1988.
54. Carver, *Elephant*, p. 117.
55. Raymond Carver, *A New Path to the Waterfall* (Collins Harvill, 1989), p. 154.

3
Anne Tyler

Anne Tyler is an example of that rare phenomenon, the writer who combines genuine popular success—her books invariably reach the top of the best seller lists in the U.S.—with real critical acclaim (she has won both the Pulitzer Prize for Literature and the National Book Critics Circle Award). This is both gratifying and understandable: her novels are engrossing, moving, enchanting and very funny, and each book contains a memorable cast of characters, drawn with enormous affection and wisdom. In a sense Tyler writes the kind of fiction that is almost impervious to critical analysis, and reviews of her work tend to confirm this. They are usually ecstatic (Diane Johnson's review of *The Accidental Tourist*, discussed in the essay on Bobbie Ann Mason in this book, is a notable exception), but reviewers allow their enthusiasm to take the form of whole-hearted, almost desperate recommendation, rather than any form of percipient analysis of Tyler's writing. (One review of *The Accidental Tourist* contains, rather alarmingly, the expression 'Words fail me', although this proves emphatically not to be the case.) My intention here, then, is to provide some sort of overview of Tyler's recent work, and to look beyond the brilliance of these novels towards their recurring themes.

Several of the author's novels over the last few years have been at least partly set in her home town of Baltimore, Maryland. Baltimore seems to inspire this kind of loyalty in its creative inhabitants: film directors John Walters and Barry Levinson have used the city for much of their work (Walters' *Hairspray*, for example, and Levinson's *Diner* and *Tin Men*). Those whose knowledge of the city is based on these fictional portrayals are unlikely to be left with any firm idea of the character of the city, however. The films referred to above are all set in the early '60s; *Hairspray* deals with the non-specific problem of racial segregation, *Diner* with a group of young men about to grow up, *Tin Men* with the fraudulent operations of the city's salesmen. And Tyler's novels are in no meaningful sense 'about' the city; her predominantly middle- or lower-middle-class characters just happen to live there.

This absence of any real portrayal of place is in itself important. Many of the other writers discussed elsewhere in this book have made attempts to come to terms with the demands of topography which inevitably accompany realist fiction; thus we talk about Bobbie Ann Mason's Kentucky, Richard Ford's Deep South (or his New Jersey suburbia), Raymond Carver's mid-west, Tama Janowitz's New York. These associations are not without their problems, however, and I have argued elsewhere that Mason's work in particular has suffered from its strong sense of place, in that critics have been quick to pigeon-hole (and diminish) her work as some kind of rural satire. But Baltimore's size (it is neither large nor small), its geographical location (neither North nor South—in Tyler's 1982 novel *Dinner at the Homesick Restaurant*, two of the characters debate whether the North or the South is the better place to live, 'till it emerged that Pearly was assuming Baltimore was North and Cody was assuming it was South'[1]), its 'standard' mix of classes and races seems to have allowed Tyler (and Levinson and Walters) to avoid having to confront their environment. Tyler's work is not urban, in the way that we have come to understand urban fiction (*The Bonfire of the Vanities, Bright Lights, Big City*), nor is it rural (Mason, Jim Harrison); Tyler's Baltimore novels are quite simply about people.

That is not to say that Baltimore fulfils no function in the books, and that location is immaterial. It is interesting, for example, that their titles frequently refer either to a notion either of home or of travel (*Dinner at the Homesick Restaurant, Celestial Navigation, The Accidental Tourist, Searching for Caleb*); as we shall see, both of these ostensibly opposing ideas are central themes of the books, and Baltimore is highly significant to this broader concept of geography. To many of

Tyler's characters, Baltimore is home, not only literally but metaphorically, and its various metaphorical meanings are worth examining.

Jeremy Pauling, for example, in *Celestial Navigation*, has for many years been literally, physically, unable to leave his 'island', the block on which his house is situated. In the opening chapter of the book his sister Amanda, suddenly realizing that Jeremy has isolated himself in this way, attempts to make him cross his self-imposed boundaries simply by marching him up the street:

> Then I gave him a prod in the side, just to get him going, and he crumpled up. Just crumpled in upon himself and folded onto the sidewalk, where he sat in a heap and shook all over. . . . His face was yellowish and his mouth hung open. . . .[2]

This kind of tragi-comic set piece is typical in Tyler's fiction, as is the intensely physical definition of home and belonging. In Jeremy's case, obviously, his self-anchoring in a tiny square of the city is indicative of an extreme inadequacy, and there is a sense in which *Celestial Navigation* is about his relationship with the physical world.

From the moment that Tyler describes his unfortunate journey away from his block, we are aware that this relationship is a problematic one. Jeremy, we are told, dreads

> using the telephone, answering the doorbell, opening mail, leaving his house, making purchases. Also wearing new clothes, standing in open spaces, meeting the eyes of a stranger, eating in the presence of others, turning on electrical appliances.[3]

Much of life is quite beyond him. His income is provided by the lodgers who share his large, run-down house (inherited from his mother); food is purchased from the one shop on the block, and other necessities are ordered by mail, or brought home by the paying guests. He has effectively cut off the outside world altogether.

He does, however, enjoy a complex relationship with representations of the physical world through his art, which consists initially (in his sister's critical words) of 'little people made of triangles of wrapping paper and diamonds of silk'.

Amanda recognizes that 'All his eye for detail goes into cutting and pasting. There is none left for real life.'[4] This observation is not strictly accurate: his collages are successful, both artistically and later commercially, precisely because of his attention to the detail of real life. Indeed, it is suggested that his handicap is caused by his ability to see life much too clearly,

> in a series of flashes, startling moments so brief that they could arrest a motion in mid-air. Like photographs, they were handed to him at unexpected times, introduced by a neutral voice: Here is where you are now. Take a look. Between flashes, he drifted into darkness. He drifted in a daze, wondering what he had seen.[5]

It is these flashes that he recreates in his work (Miss Vinton, one of the lodgers, describes his subjects as 'the smallest and most unnoticed scenes on earth'[6]), and he uses the very stuff of life—bus tickets and book covers and pieces of old tin—to capture them. It is not that he is unable to make a link with the world; simply that he has to take a complicated route through to it.

The events that unfold during the course of the novel require Jeremy to readjust these visions and connexions. Firstly, he falls in love with one of the lodgers, Mary Tell, a single parent who has been abandoned by her lover; they set up house together (Mary is not initially free to marry), and they produce a number of children. Like Jeremy, Mary is essentially bound to the block, but for different reasons: she cannot go far from her small daughter, she is poor, and takes on piece-work at home in an attempt to pay her rent. This coincidence is only a superficial bond, in that Mary, unlike Jeremy, has not sought her exclusion from the rest of the city, yet it is enough to give substance to their partnership; but when Jeremy forgets their wedding day, Mary leaves him and takes the children with her.

During the course of these upheavals, Jeremy's art, the system he has devised through necessity to anchor himself into the world, begins to change its form. When he becomes aware of his love for Mary, he becomes dissatisfied with his collages:

Nowadays [they] filled him with impatience. He became conscious of the way his eyes tightened and ached when he looked at them too long. He started wishing for more structure, things standing out for themselves. . . . Not a sculpture, exactly. He shied away from anything that loomed so.[7]

He begins to use 'actual objects—thumbtacks and washers and bits of string and wood'[8]; and later, at the time Mary leaves, he is after all involved with something that 'looms': a sculpture of a friend 'rounding the corner—a man half running, glad to be gone'.[9] This is the only outward evidence that Jeremy has begun to reconcile himself to his dramatic new environment; when Miss Vinton expresses her regret that Jeremy has not complimented his wife on a new dress, Mary explains that she knows Jeremy loves it because he has 'cut a patch from inside the hem and used it for one of his pieces'.[10] Significantly, it is because he is so intensely involved in the sculpture that he provokes Mary into leaving him; he is unable to assimilate his metaphorical involvement with the world into his literal involvement.

The book's final sections makes Jeremy's struggle for physical orientation more explicit. Olivia, a young, callow student whom Mary has brought into the house, endeavours to substitute herself for Mary in Jeremy's affections; but she does so by attempting to become a part of his world, rather than confront him, as Mary did, with life and noise and the banalities of everyday existence. The results are disastrous, because without the firm moorings that Mary provided, Jeremy floats away from the real world altogether, and Olivia's desire to understand and maybe share in his creative process results in the two of them effectively living inside Jeremy's head:

> I taught him to sleep late. Waking, finding me beside him, he would struggle up. 'Be still', I said, and he lay down again and stared, as I did, at the towering white ceiling while noon approached and rolled over us and rumbled away again. Now I was an artist too. In my mind I colored the ceiling with the jagged lightning bolts you see when you squinch your eyes tight; so did Jeremy. We did it together. No strings snagged us to the rest of the world.[11]

Olivia contrasts her own willingness to abandon reality with Mary's firm sense of self-orientation. The younger woman recollects watching Mary serenely crossing the road with her brood, and wonders: 'What do you suppose it feels like to be so certain of your rôle? To have such a clear sense of place?'[12] These are questions central to the theme of the book, and Olivia's reference to a 'sense of place' is a summation of what separates Mary and Jeremy; whereas Mary is capable of orienting herself practically and immediately in any circumstance, Jeremy operates, as Miss Vinton recognizes, by 'celestial navigation'.[13]

Tyler's most extraordinary achievement in *Celestial Navigation* is to take the form of the domestic novel and stretch its limits. The author's self-imposed limitations—her invention dictates that her narrative can step outside the confines of Jeremy's house only for one brief section at the end of the book—are severe; and yet in Olivia's section of the novel Tyler manages to push domesticity into the realms of the metaphysical by providing an account of a man whose fear of his surroundings forces an extreme retreat. Tyler's usual skills—her characterization, her revelatory plotting, her hallmark combination of humour and pathos—are as evident as elsewhere in her work, but *Celestial Navigation* contains a quiet experimentation unique in contemporary main-stream fiction.

In Tyler's 1976 novel *Searching for Caleb* Baltimore transforms itself into another metaphor, with a meaning almost diametrically opposed to that revealed in *Celestial Navigation*. In the latter novel, the city's size and life threatens the central character to the extent that he suffers a kind of paralysis; in the former, the central couple, Justine and Duncan Peck, escape from Baltimore because it is too small, and its tameness stifles.

The Peck clan (Duncan and Justine are married cousins) are representatives of Baltimore's vanishing upper-middle class; this is the only novel in which Tyler touches upon the city's old-rich families. (When we are provided with a brief history of the Peck wealth, which has its origins in the 1870s, Baltimore society is described as 'narrow and ossified even then'.[14]) Most of the Pecks are mildly snobbish, gently pretentious, cocooned from the real world; Duncan, who feels alienated from the family and all it stands for, provides a memorable list of their affectations:

> And we've all been taught that we disapprove of sports cars, golf, women in slacks, chewing gum, the color chartreuse, emotional displays, ranch houses, bridge, mascara, household pets, religious discussions, plastic, politics, nail polish, transparent gems of any color, jewelry shaped like animals, checkered prints. . . .[15]

In *Searching for Caleb*, Baltimore becomes for Duncan a physical manifestation of Peckishness, and he must distance himself from it. Yet he, like the rest of the central characters in the book, and so many of Tyler's other characters, is still defined by his relationship with Baltimore, with home, and thus in many ways the novel is about how one comes to terms with one's physical and emotional centre.

The narrative structure of *Searching for Caleb* is Tyler's most ambitious and epic to date, spanning as it does four generations and several states, and featuring a bewildering cast of characters. The Caleb of the title is the great-uncle of Justine and Duncan, who disappeared in 1912; the novel is an account both of Grandfather Peck's decades-long hunt for his brother and of the marriage of his two grandchildren.

On the face of it this is an unwieldy combination, but it is Baltimore, or rather, its absence from the lives of these characters, that links the two strands together. Caleb's disappearance, like Duncan's some fifty years later, is a reaction to the ossification and narrowness of his immediate surroundings; when Caleb eventually resurfaces, he forges an immediate bond with Duncan, and his spheres of experience are notably unPecklike:

> Duncan would ask about Lafleur Boudrault, and Whisky Alley, and musical funerals and old-time cathouses, about which (Justine was surprised to hear) Caleb seemed to know everything. Caleb played Duncan's harmonica, drawing forth from it such beautiful, disreputable sounds that Justine stood motionless and open-mouthed. *This* was her great-*uncle*?[16]

Whereas Caleb has been to New Orleans and earned a living as an itinerant musician, and Duncan travels from town to town with his wife and daughter, picking up new skills as he goes, the generation between them—Duncan's parents and their brothers and sisters—are almost as afraid of the world outside Baltimore as Jeremy Pauling. When they set off on an expedition to visit Duncan and Justine, some two hours out of the city, they take with them

> presents and fruit, a Thermos of Sanka, Laura May's needlework, Sarah's knitting, insect repellent, sun-screen, Bufferin, Gelusil, a Triple-A tour guide, a can of Fix-a-Flat, a fire extinguisher, six emergency flares, and a white banner reading SEND HELP.[17]

With the arrival of Meg, Duncan's daughter, a formal generational pattern seems to have emerged; each alternate generation reacts against the excesses of the first. Where Duncan and to a lesser extent Justine reacted against the constrictions of their parents, whose helplessness is exemplified in the above passage, Meg reacts against her parents' inability to provide a conventional home for her:

> She ironed her own dresses, as she had since she was nine. (Justine thought there was no point in ironing, as long as things were clean.) At the age of ten, she baked her first cake, which everyone admired but no one ate because they were too busy rushing off somewhere. . . . 'Oh, I just love your folks,' girls were always saying, little dreaming what agony it would be to have them for their own.[18]

Meg rediscovers Peckishness, whereas Duncan and Caleb are anti-Peck; one of the themes of the book is that this kind of automatic reflex reaction against the sins, or rather the excesses, of the parents—a rejection of the concept of home, or an over-enthusiastic acceptance of it—results in, at worst, unhappiness, or at best a kind of shiftlessness and permanent immaturity. Meg's desire for a permanent home, and her (understandably) narrow understanding of what domesticity entails, ends in an unhappy marriage to a pinched but thoroughly unadventurous clergyman; Caleb's self-imposed separation from his real family, it transpires, has put him at the mercy of surrogate offspring who use their lack of blood ties as a pretext for putting him in a bleak state institution.

Duncan's rootlessness is less dramatically self-destructive. The end of each career he has chosen for himself—antiques dealer, record-store manager, farmer—is marked by a mild flirtation with alcohol and a sudden disinterest in the job at hand, during which states he allows the businesses to go to ruin. The pay-off is that he is unable to grow up; at his grandfather's funeral, both his wife and his relatives realize how the years have left no mark on him:

> 'My,' they said to Justine, 'are *you* that little girl of Caroline's? But you used to be so—well, you certainly have—now this is your husband, isn't it? *Him* I recognize.'
> . . . 'Why, Duncan!' said Justine, dropping her glove. 'You haven't changed a bit.'[19]

There are, of course, obvious advantages to this state of eternal youth, but in the context of the novel it is for the most part one of Duncan's more unattractive features, despite his boyish charm. Given the ridiculous inadequacy of his parents and his aunts and uncles, it is ironic and significant that his youthfulness results in a strong similarity to the despised generation above him: as they grow older, the lines in 'their curiously innocent faces' make them resemble 'aging midgets'[20]; and at the funeral, Justine makes the connection between her husband and his parents: 'Not only had Duncan remained the same but so had her aunts and uncles.'[21] Ultimately, neither side has allowed themselves to live a life which admits maturity.

Justine, however, who like her grandfather, through choice and circumstance has come to rest somewhere between the warring factions, recognizes that ageing is both necessary and desirable. When her daughter elopes, she is desperately hurt:

> But then I looked up, and there I was reflected in the window that was just starting to grow dark outside. There were these deep black shadows in my eyes and cheekbones. I thought, 'My, don't I look interesting? Like someone who has had something *dramatic* happen.'[22]

Duncan's determination to avoid routine, and his parents' determination to avoid the outside world, are the cause of an stuntedness which has a physical manifestation; Justine's self-perception and her ability to confront pain is by implication much healthier.

Both Justine and her grandfather, the other 'non-aligned' character, are at heart Pecks whose desires (Justine's love for Duncan, her grandfather's need to find Caleb) involve adaptation to different circumstances. Grandfather's idea of an after-life is the vision of an unreconstructed Peck:

> I would prefer to find that heaven was a small town with a bandstand in the park and a great many trees, and I would know everybody in it and none of them would ever die or move away or age or alter.[23]

Moving away, of course, is a particularly undesirable thing to do, if one is a Peck (the novel opens with a journey—Justine and Grandfather Peck chasing up a lead towards Caleb that like all the others comes to nothing—and a diatribe from the old man on the foolishness of leaving Baltimore). And yet he is prepared to travel, in an attempt to find Caleb. There is even a suspicion that he has come to accept his new itinerant life-style; when one of his daughters comes to visit,

> she wondered if he didn't almost *enjoy* this life—these dismal houses, weird friends, separations from the family, this moving about and fortune telling. If he weren't almost proud of the queer situations he found himself in.[24]

This pride is suddenly dented by a reference to home—'Grandma's orange peel cake'—and his face becomes 'suddenly thin and lost'.[25] But there is in this passage an unstated sense of life's paradoxes: that humans possess the need both to travel and to retain roots, to move on and to stay behind. Grandfather and Justine both come to understand that whereas a 'proper' home in the Baltimore sense of the word is not always possible if one is to live a complete life, a nostalgia for home is both unavoidable and desirable. Duncan and his parents are aware of only half of the equation.

Grandfather's remaining traces of Peckishness cost him the realization of his dream of finding his brother; when Caleb is eventually traced, Grandfather writes him a letter exhibiting all his family's petty snobbery and inability to comprehend any kind of non-Baltimore life-style, and Caleb does not reply. (It is this snobbery, ironically, which has prevented the family from finding Caleb; the private detective who succeeds where they have failed began his search by asking their maid, who was able to provide a vital clue—the Pecks, of course, had not bothered with her.)

Justine, however, is less steeped in the Peck ethos, and

manages to find a way to synthesize the elements in her nature which would otherwise similarly prevent her from fulfilment. The novel ends with Justine and Duncan preparing to go on the road with a travelling fun fair, where Justine can tell fortunes and Duncan can utilize his mechanical skills; it is a decision which counterbalances Justine's recognition of the necessity for roots (the narrative tricks us into believing initially that Duncan and Justine are returning to Baltimore, where Justine could survive but where her husband would suffocate) and Duncan's desire to move, since the couple will henceforward be surrounded by a permanent travelling 'family'.

Like *Celestial Navigation, Searching for Caleb* is more than a domestic novel; it is a meditation on the nature of domesticity, on our understanding of what home means, and on how a partial grasp of its importance can be destructive. Once more, Baltimore serves as much more than a setting: the city is a character with as much power to act and to influence as any of Tyler's people.

The titles of Tyler's first two novels of the '80s, *Dinner at the Homesick Restaurant* and *The Accidental Tourist* (both, again, set firmly in Baltimore), refer to attempts to recreate home. The Homesick Restaurant is Ezra Tull's vision of a home away from home, an eaterie that offers a bewildering variety of nourishing fare 'cooked with love'. *The Accidental Tourist* is the generic title of Macon Leary's series of travel guides, written for the traveller who wishes only the bare minimum of disruption to his usual domestic routine:

> What hotels in Madrid boasted king-sized Beautyrest mattresses? What restaurants in Tokyo offered Sweet'n'Low? Did Amsterdam have a McDonald's? Did Mexico City have a Taco Bell? Did any place in Rome offer Chef Boyardee ravioli? Other travelers hoped to discover distinctive local wines; Macon's readers searched for pasteurized and homogenised milk.[26]

What becomes clear in the novels is that the central characters are essentially dealing with a *myth* of home; the domestic reality of both the Tull family and Macon Leary is somewhat different, and these enterprises serve a compensatory purpose.

Dinner at the Homesick Restaurant begins with Pearl Tull's dying moments, and then proceeds to recount in a series of flashbacks her life as a single parent (like many of Tyler's women characters—Mary Tell, Muriel in *The Accidental Tourist*—Pearl is abandoned by her husband while she has young children to care for), before describing the complicated network of relationships between her adult children, their spouses and her grandchildren. The novel is, then, a family saga in its purest form, and it is thus unsurprising that it should provide Tyler's most direct contemplations on the meaning of home.

Tyler's *modus operandi* in the novel is to provide some kind of central truth about the Tull family from which its members extract memories and messages they later use to guide their lives. This truth, Tyler seems to be saying, is that their experiences are relatively commonplace: moments of real savagery and unkindness and heartbreak, intertwined with the humdrum and, less occasionally, pleasantness and calm. And yet it is not a truth that the children can understand. When Cody Tull looks back on family life with his father, he remembers only

> meals shattered with quarrels, other meals disrupted when Ezra spilled his milk, drives in the country where his father lost the way and his mother snapped out pained and exasperated directions.[27]

Episodes recounted by the author in a third person unfiltered through memory show Cody's loathing for his father; on a trip to the country Cody watches Beck Tull and decides that 'he looked like a fool.' And yet after Beck has disappeared Cody takes his friends into his mother's bedroom and shows them items of jewellery he claims Pearl's husband has bought for her: ' "He thinks a lot of her," he would say. "He's given her heaps of stuff. Heaps. There's heaps of other stuff that I just don't happen to have on hand." '[28]

This kind of mythologizing is repeated throughout Cody's adolescence and adulthood. In the novel's central episode, Cody succeeds in stealing his brother's fiancée away from him and marrying her himself, not only because of his long-felt resentment towards Ezra, but because of the character and appearance of the girl. Ruth, a member of Ezra's restaurant staff, is 'a weasel-faced little redhead', with hair 'cut so short that it seemed too scant for her skull'[29]; Cody notices that she has 'no hips whatsoever'[30] and that she is wearing jeans bought in a store for boys. Her sexlessness makes her a surprising choice for Cody, who has a history of involvement with glamorous women; but Pearl's description of Ruth as 'homely' is perhaps the closest definition of the cause of Cody's infatuation. Ruth thus perfectly exemplifies the duality in Cody's obsession with home: one half of his desire for her stems from his belief in the myth of perfect domesticity (he goes so far as to buy a farmhouse for him and his new wife to live in, but cannot bring himself to move into it, and leaves it empty, to be maintained by Ezra and Pearl); yet the other half stems from one the realities of his home life—his bitter feelings for his brother.

Jenny, Pearl's daughter, is similarly driven to strive for some kind of idealized marriage, to the extent that over the course of the novel she marries three times. The first, Harley, is a kind of sanitized husband, an arid intellectual who brushes off the soles of his feet before getting into bed with her; the second, 'the one she'd loved the best', sees Jenny veering off into the other direction: 'she'd made a fool of herself over Sam'[31]; Joe, the third, has several children from a previous marriage, and Jenny's relationship with him seems simply to fulfil her need for a ready-made 'perfect' family.

Even the children of these marriages are disturbed by the absence of a home in the absolutely standard sense of the word. Jenny's stepson Slevin steals Pearl's Hoover, apparently in an attempt to capture the spirit of his absent mother; Cody's son Luke hitch-hikes back to Baltimore, where he presumes he will somehow find the familial warmth in his uncle and grandmother that he cannot find in his parents' loveless marriage. (Both of the people who give him lifts on his journey are in different ways attempting to rebuild shattered home lives: a mother with a monstrous adolescent daughter driving around aimlessly—'it's like I'm driving till I find her past self. . . . And *my* past self',[32] she tells Luke; and a recently divorced teacher touring the country with his young son and a list of school-era old girl-friends. The whole world, apparently, is on the highways of America looking for a past they have lost or that they never had.)

It is Ezra and his restaurant, though, that provide the novel with its narrative and thematic centre. As pointed out above, the Homesick Restaurant is a neat summation of the ambitions and delusions of Pearl's children. Where Jenny chooses children as her (inappropriate) symbol for home, and Cody chooses Ruth, for Ezra it is food. Again, it is a grossly idealized approximation of his own familial experience; his mother

> burned things you would not imagine it possible to burn and served others half-raw, adding jarring extras of her own design such as crushed pineapple in the mashed potatoes. . . . Her only seasonings were salt and pepper. Her only gravy was Campbell's cream of mushroom soup, undiluted.[33]

Ezra's conception of a restaurant where the food will be 'solid and wholesome, really homelike' is thus hardly an accurate approximation of the Tull family kitchen, and his choice of name is perhaps much more meaningful than he had intended; he is nostalgic for a conception of home that he has never known.

Ezra compounds these delusions by insisting throughout the novel on gathering the Tulls together for large family dinners which invariably end in disaster, with one family member storming out as a reaction to some real or perceived insult. Instead of emphasizing the self-sufficiency of the family, these dinners seem to accentuate its inadequacy, as Jenny observes:

> These three young people and this shrunken mother, she thought, were not enough to sustain the occasion. They could have used several more members—a family clown, for instance; and a genuine black sheep, blacker than Cody; and maybe one of those managerial older sisters who holds a group together by force. As things were, it was Ezra who had to hold them together. He wasn't doing a very good job.[34]

There is another explicit contrast between the myth of the family and the reality of the Tulls in the book's closing scene—a family dinner after Pearl's funeral, to which Ezra has invited Beck, absent for thirty years or more. Beck is amazed and gratified by the way the family has grown: 'it looks like this is one of those great big, jolly, noisy, rambling

... why, *families!*'³⁵ Cody, however, is quick to disabuse him:

> Don't let them mislead you. It's not the way it appears. ...
> You think we're a family. ... You think we're some jolly, situation comedy family when we're in particles, torn apart, torn all over the place, and our mother was a witch.³⁶

Cody's view of his mother is important, because Pearl is the link between all the characters at the table, and his condemnation brings the book towards a coherent conclusion. Certainly Pearl is capable of enormous cruelty:

> Which of her children had not felt her stinging slap, with the claw-encased pearl in her engagement ring that could bloody a lip at one flick? Jenny had seen her hurl Cody down a flight of stairs. She'd seen Ezra ducking, elbows raised, warding off an attack. She herself, more than once, had been slammed against a wall, been called 'serpent', 'cockroach', 'hideous little sniveling guttersnipe'.³⁷

And yet it is Pearl who has the clearest understanding both of herself and what it means to be a part of the family. 'I know you must think I'm difficult,' she tells Cody.

> I lose my temper, I carry on like a shrew sometimes, but if you could just realize how ... helpless I feel! How scary it is to know that everyone I love depends on me! I'm afraid I'll do something wrong.³⁸

This kind of self-awareness has been denied to her children, to varying extents; they persist in striving for a domestic perfection that they feel they have been denied but which in reality is denied to everybody. At the final dinner at the Homesick Restaurant, it is Beck who storms out, goaded by Cody's insults. When Cody catches up with him, his father provides a succinct encapsulation of the book's predominant concerns while trying to articulate what it was that made him walk out on his family:

> See, ... what it was, I guess: it was the grayness; grayness of things; half-right-and-half-wrongness of things. Everything, tangled, mingled, not perfect any more. I couldn't take that. Your mother could, but not me. Yes sir, I have to hand it to your mother.³⁹

Beck can understand the 'half-right-and-half-wrongness of things', but cannot accept it; his children, over the course of the novel, show again and again that they have not even learned to understand it.

The Accidental Tourist completes this quartet of novels dealing with domestic neurosis. The Leary family—the travel writer Macon, his brothers Charles and Porter, and his sister Rose—have characteristics which recall those of both the Pecks and Jeremy Pauling. Like the Pecks, the Learys share an overwhelming family ethos which makes them more or less interchangeable. They have an obsession with order and routine; and, like both the Pecks and the central character of *Celestial Navigation*, any trip away from home base, however local, results in complete disorientation:

> It was a kind of dyslexia, Macon believed—a geographic dyslexia. None of them ever stepped outside without noting all available landmarks, clinging to a fixed and desperate mental map of the neighbourhood.[40]

Macon Leary's profession as travel-writer for those who have no real desire to leave home is thus perfect: he has a career based around this 'geographic dyslexia', and each trip abroad is shaped by his anxious search for American breakfasts and American mattresses and American hamburgers. Yet whereas many of the Tyler characters previously examined in this essay suffer from their inability to adjust to new circumstances, Macon Leary's neuroses stem from his ability to adjust absolutely and completely to any new situation, however alien, however painful.

The Accidental Tourist is in many ways Tyler's most conventional love story, as the bulk of its narrative is taken up with Macon's relationship with Muriel, a chaotic and, crucially, working-class single parent whose grim determination to survive entails a number of jobs, including that of dog-trainer; when Macon's dog Edward starts to get out of hand, he is forced to employ Muriel, and their affair begins. For Macon, however, the relationship has its roots in the recent past: in the novel's opening, his wife Sarah asks for a divorce, apparently because Macon has been unable to react properly to the death of his young son Ethan, murdered senselessly during a hold-up in a hamburger restaurant. He responds inappropriately (he appears not to have mourned, in the accepted sense of the word, and rarely talks of the incident to his wife), not because he cannot confront his grief, but because he has equipped himself to survive anything, with a minimum of psychic disturbance. 'Everything that might touch you or upset you or disrupt you, you've given up without a murmur and done without, said you never wanted it anyhow,' Sarah tells him[41]; later, Macon recalls watching Ethan run into the street after a ball as a pick-up truck came hurtling towards him:

> In one split second he adjusted to a future that held no Ethan—an immeasurably bleaker place, but also, by way of compensation, plainer and simpler. . . . Then the truck stopped short and Ethan retrieved his ball, and Macon's knees went weak with relief. But he remembered forever after how quickly he had adjusted. . . . But if people didn't adjust, how could they bear to go on?[42]

When we are told that Macon 'approved of planes. When the weather was calm, you couldn't even tell you were moving',[43] the detail makes perfect sense; he has found a way to travel through his life in exactly the same way.

In part, then, the novel is in itself an answer to Macon's rhetorical question quoted above: paradoxically it is an account of a man who has to lose his inbuilt survival mechanisms in order to survive. When Sarah leaves him, it soon becomes clear that Macon's life is an existence, but no more: his adjustments to life without his wife are designed to make life easier, but they simultaneously remove any sense of variety or pleasure. He replaces meals with the odd glass of milk or spoonful of ice cream when he becomes hungry, and starts wearing sweat-suits which can serve as both day and night wear. This life-style contains within it the seeds of its own destruction: a particularly complicated energy-saving idea involving a skateboard and the cellar results in Macon breaking his leg, and he returns to the Leary family home to live with his unmarried sister Rose and his brothers, one of whom has also returned after a failed marriage. Certainly Macon has the ability to adjust; but the adjustments he makes are to the rhythms of his own life rather than to other people or to exterior circumstances, and his behaviour post-Sarah, pre-Muriel is an extreme form of solipsism. When he returns to the family home, he has no further need for adaptation of any kind: he is wifeless, childless, and once more playing endless games of 'Inoculation', a card game invented by the Learys whose rules are so complicated that only family members can understand them—a typically concise and witty Tyler metaphor. It is Muriel—inevitably and perhaps predictably the polar opposite of Macon—who breaks the pattern.

Muriel lives on Singleton Street, in one of Baltimore's poorest areas, and this in itself requires a new awareness on Macon's part. There is little opportunity for him to pretend that he is at home:

> There were too many murky alleys and stairwells full of rubbish and doorways lined with tattered shreds of posters. The gridded shops with their ineptly lettered signs offered services that had a sleazy ring to them: CHECKS CASHED NO QUESTIONS, TINY BUBBA'S INCOME TAX, SAME DAY AUTO RECOLORING.[44]

It is entirely typical of the Tyler *oeuvre* that Macon's journey towards some kind of psychic wholeness should be provoked by a move away from home: 'In the foreign country that was Singleton Street he was an entirely different person.'[45] Muriel's neighbourhood is Tyler's first real foray outside Baltimore's middle class (even Jeremy Pauling's boarding-house is home to a very genteel set of guests), but as always the topographical reality is hardly crucial to the meaning of the novel; Singleton Street is simply a new and hitherto unsuspected area of Macon's psyche.

It is worth noting at this point the extraordinary similarity between the central narrative of *The Accidental Tourist* and an important section of Richard Ford's *The Sportswriter*. Both books (and they were published within months of each other) are about writers of one kind or another; each of these writers has suffered the death of a young son, and each has separated from his wife as an indirect result of their tragedies. Both of them then take up with apparently unsuitable women from a different class; and both Ford and Tyler describe the meetings between the man and his new girl-friend's mother and father (Macon spends Christmas Day with Muriel's parents, and Frank Bascombe spends Thanksgiving with Vicky's). Admittedly the relationships are of a very different order, and Bascombe's dalliance with Vicky fails miserably; but it is interesting that two very different writers from a country which has occasionally trumpeted its own classlessness should hit upon cross-class love affairs as a metaphor for their central characters' spiritual bewilderment.

Macon's new circumstances amid the human flotsam and jetsam on Singleton Street, then, require a radical reorientation on his part. But the most significant relationship in the novel is not between Macon and Singleton Street, or Macon and Muriel but between Macon and Alexander, Muriel's sickly son. Macon begins with the straightforward physical details of surrogate fatherhood: he teaches him how to change a washer, helps him with his homework, and so on. Yet

> There was a peculiar kind of luxury here: Alexander was not his own child. Macon felt linked to him in all sorts of complicated ways, but not in that inseparable, inevitable way that he'd been linked to Ethan. He could still draw back from Alexander; he could still give up on him.[46]

In Macon's experience, the ultimate adjustment is to one's own child; Ethan prevented him from indulging in the solipsism he has constructed since the boy's death. Alexander is not his own, and therefore Macon feels that further reorientation is superfluous. Later, however, in a pivotal episode, Macon steps in to prevent Alexander from being bullied by neighbourhood children, and when the boy clutches his hand as they return to the house, he realizes that giving up and drawing back may not be possible after all:

> Macon tightened his grip and felt a pleasant kind of sorrow sweeping through him. Oh, his life had regained all its old perils. He was forced to worry once again about nuclear war and the future of the planet. He often had the same secret, guilty thought that had come to him after Ethan was born: *From this time on I can never be completely happy.*[47]

At the book's conclusion, Macon finds himself having to choose between this 'pleasant kind of sorrow' and the kind of vacant contentment he had constructed for himself after his son's death. (This vacancy is emphasized by a dream in which Macon finds himself a suspect at the scene of a crime; 'You have to see my side of this!' he finds himself shouting to his accusers. 'I put it all out of my mind; I worked to put it out! Now I can't bring it back.'[48] Sarah finds that she actually prefers the numbness of her life with Macon, and they effect a trial reconciliation; but Macon opts for potential pain and sadness, and returns to Muriel and her son. *The Accidental Tourist* is thus Tyler's most life-affirming work; and its strength lies in its emotional complexity, its ability to reach its conclusion without simplification (Sarah remains a sympathetic character throughout the novel, and their final separation is difficult), sentimentality or triumphalism. It is a touching conclusion to an extraordinary quartet.

Anne Tyler is actually the least 'contemporary' of any of the writers discussed in this book; her first novel was published over twenty-five years ago, and thus by rights should belong to a different generation, with different concerns. In fact, her work is a central reference point for both the 'Dirty Realists' and the *New Yorker*-style short-story writers: her use of brand names, for example, and her references to popular culture, foreshadows Bobbie Ann Mason's attempts to place her characters within modern American society; and her concentration on the domestic paved the way for Ann Beattie and Elizabeth Tallent. She is a writer who has *become* contemporary (her preoccupations were far from modish in the 1960s and '70s): the four novels discussed here rank alongside Ford's *The Sportswriter* as among the finest in post-war American literature.

NOTES

1. Anne Tyler, *Dinner at the Homesick Restaurant* (Penguin, 1983), p. 251.
2. Anne Tyler, *Celestial Navigation* (Pavanne, 1988), p. 39.
3. Ibid., p. 86.
4. Ibid., p. 24.
5. Ibid., p. 43.
6. Ibid., p. 145.
7. Ibid., p. 90.

8. Ibid., p. 114.
9. Ibid., p. 181.
10. Ibid., p. 144.
11. Ibid., pp. 242–43.
12. Ibid., p. 228.
13. Ibid., p. 145.
14. Anne Tyler, *Searching for Caleb* (Pavanne, 1988), p. 50.
15. Ibid., pp. 88–9.
16. Ibid., p. 289.
17. Ibid., p. 196.
18. Ibid., p. 164.
19. Ibid., p. 255.
20. Ibid., p. 148.
21. Ibid., p. 255.
22. Ibid., p. 195.
23. Ibid., p. 190.
24. Ibid., p. 202.
25. Ibid., p. 202.
26. Anne Tyler, *The Accidental Tourist* (Penguin, 1986), p. 12.
27. Tyler, *Dinner at the Homesick Restaurant*, p. 40.
28. Ibid., p. 48.
29. Ibid., p. 139.
30. Ibid., p. 147.
31. Ibid., p. 207.
32. Ibid., p. 241.
33. Ibid., p. 160.
34. Ibid., pp. 107–8.
35. Ibid., p. 294.
36. Ibid., p. 294.
37. Ibid., p. 70.
38. Ibid., p. 63.
39. Ibid., p. 301.
40. Tyler, *The Accidental Tourist*, p. 116.
41. Ibid, p. 141.
42. Ibid., p. 143.
43. Ibid., p. 30.
44. Ibid., p. 198.
45. Ibid., p. 212.
46. Ibid., pp. 237–38.
47. Ibid., p. 258.
48. Ibid., p. 324.

4
Bobbie Ann Mason

Of all the writers who are featured in *Granta*'s two 'Dirty Realism' collections, it is Bobbie Ann Mason who continues to cause British literary critics the most trouble. Here are some recent reactions to *Love Life*, her second collection of short stories, and *Spence + Lila*, a novella, published simultaneously in 1989 in Britain:

> Not much happens in Paducah, the fictional Kentucky town where most of Bobbie Ann Mason's stories and novels are set. It is a small world where the little things count. The tentative affair in the cheap motel, the quiet moments of nostalgia about life before the invasion of shopping malls and cable TV, the private dreams of country music stardom—Mason writes about Southerners who enjoy life's small pleasures because they are the only ones they are going to get.[1]

> What keeps one reading is not always the empathy with plain folks, but more the sense that one is enjoying sleuthing in Hicksville in the company of a practised satirical eavesdropper. . . . A reader can be forgiven, by the fifteenth story, for regarding them as the same characters recycled under fifteen different names. But then, the names themselves are a cornucopia—Kerry, Tammy, Jolene, Shayla.[2]

> Critics have compared her to Raymond Carver and John Updike, but I cannot appreciate this kind of reading of Mason's work. . . . Mason in my opinion has more in common with Virginia Woolf than with Anne Tyler.[3]

The most immediately noticeable feature of these passages

is the bewildering range of writers to whom Mason is compared, both expressly and implicitly (the first two reviews would seem to be pointing us towards Garrison Keiller's Lake Woebegone stories). What is one to make of an author whose work is at once reminiscent of Carver and Woolf, and by implication Updike and Tyler?

Also apparent is the distance between English reviewers and the writer, and the assumed distance between Mason and her characters. If we were to read an American review of an English novel which began 'Not much happens in Norwich, the fictional Norfolk town. . .', we would perhaps begin to question the critic's qualifications for the job. Yet Paducah is not a fictional town, and mistakes of this kind in responses to Mason's work seem to reveal a central problem in the understanding of it. An American reader who is familiar with Paducah, or at least with its relevance to Mason's stories as the urban centre of an enormous rural area, will read and understand Mason's fiction in a very different way to someone who assumes the town is imaginary.

The second passage throws up a slightly different assumption, although one which connects with the misunderstanding in the first. The 'cornucopia of names' which the reviewer repeats with apparent amusement imply a condescension on Mason's part which allow her to be classed as a satirist. Yet Mason's own first names would fit into the list quite comfortably: they are just as redolent of 'Hicksville'. Though Mason chooses the names of her characters carefully, it seems unlikely that her purpose in so doing is a satirical one. This assumption to the contrary reveals more about the reviewer than it does about Mason's fiction.

What is interesting about these reactions is that they have long been familiar to a whole series of writers from the American South. Hermione Lee, in her introduction to Flannery O'Connor's *Everything that Rises Must Converge*, feels that

> English readers may have been put off by [O'Connor's] recondite titles, or even by her name, which, as with other under-valued writers of the deep South—Eudora Welty, Walker Percy—has a bizarre ring to our ears.[4]

And O'Connor herself complained:

> Any fiction that comes out of the South is going to be called grotesque by Northern readers—unless it is really grotesque. Then—it is going to be called photographic realism.[5]

Willa Cather, whose *O! Pioneers* was set in Nebraska rather than the South, recalled the reaction of a New York critic to the novel: 'I simply don't care a damn what happens in Nebraska, no matter who writes about it.'[6]

It would be surprising if this reaction were to be expressly repeated, given the lip-service that is paid on both sides of the Atlantic to a pluralism of culture at the moment. However, a review of Mason's novel *In Country* by Diane Johnson in the *New York Review of Books* refers slightingly to 'those works of fiction with their fashionable settings in rural or small-town America among lower-middle class people—what Jonathan Yardley has called "hick chic" '.[7]

The underlying sentiment here contains an echo of Willa Cather's New York critic, particularly in its suggestion that rural settings in American fiction are a fad; the extension of this is that when the fad ends, as all fads do, writers and critics will once more be able to concentrate on more enduring urban themes and settings. What will then happen to writers and critics whose background and source of inspiration is 'Hicksville', Johnson omits to say.

Johnson's review deals at the same time with Anne Tyler's *The Accidental Tourist*. Tyler's recent fiction is discussed elsewhere, but it is worth noticing that 'hick chic' can refer to Tyler's Baltimore as well as Mason's Kentucky. As Baltimore has a population of over 2,000,000, and is therefore appreciably larger than, say, Dallas, it would appear that any fiction not set in New York, Chicago or Los Angeles can be categorized as 'rural'.

Johnson argues that 'Tyler's version of Baltimore, like Mason's small town, suggests all of small, middle, rural America.'[8] This may well be the case as far as Tyler is concerned, but Mason herself has made it clear that it is certainly not her intention that her settings should be interpreted as archetypal in this way. In an interview in the *New York Times*, she explained that she had no desire to write about rural

Pennsylvania, where she now lives:

> It doesn't motivate me in the way writing about my home state does. It's a difference in the language. I don't know the language of Pennsylvania. It doesn't ring the bell that Kentucky does.[9]

To Johnson, then, Mason is writing about an all-purpose 'Hicksville' that is supposed to suggest 'all of small, middle, rural America' (an interesting juxtaposition of adjectives, recalling the film industry's term for the several thousand miles between New York and Los Angeles, 'the flyover belt'). Mason herself, however, feels that she is only capable of describing one particular region, the region where she grew up. It is clear from Mason's own words that these two conceptions are incompatible.

I do not wish to suggest (and I am sure Mason is not suggesting) that her work cannot be properly enjoyed or understood by those who have never been to West Kentucky; in fact, her work is enormously accessible. But critical attempts to dismiss regional writing as a fashion, and which wilfully misunderstand or mistake setting and intention, result in writers like Mason labouring under a considerable handicap. It would seem, from the experiences of Willa Cather and Flannery O'Connor, that rural writers have been similarly handicapped for most of this century.

'Shiloh', the title story of Mason's first collection, is in many ways an ideal introduction to her work, and its very first paragraph contains a number of typical features:

> Leroy Moffit's wife, Norma Jean, is working on her pectorals. She lifts three-pound dumbells to warm up, then progresses to a twenty-pound barbell. Standing with her legs apart, she reminds Leroy of Wonder Woman.[10]

The short sentences, the flat, colourless prose, the use of the present tense, the image drawn from American popular culture—these are characteristics not just of Bobbie Ann Mason's fiction, but of much of the new American writing.

Couples like Leroy and Norma Jean Moffit are scattered throughout these first stories. Leroy, a truck driver, has been at home for four months since being involved in a highway accident which injured his leg, and will probably not be able to return to his old work. Norma Jean, who works at the Rexall drug-store (again, brand names feature heavily in Mason's work, and I will return to this later) is uncertain about their new rôles. She 'is often startled to find Leroy at home, and he thinks she seems a little disappointed about it'.[11] While Norma Jean is out at work, Leroy sits at home 'making things from craft kits'.[12]

There is a gentle irony in the reversal, and touches like this illuminate why Mason is occasionally thought of as a satirist. Just at the point where the reader is beginning to expect a *New Yorker* cartoon portrayal of changing male/female stereotypes, however, a different note is introduced: we discover that the couple had a child who died when he was four months old. Inevitably this shifts the tone of 'Shiloh' slightly, but what gives Mason's work a distinctive voice is her refusal to alter her wry tone even after the injection of a painful and tragic circumstance of this kind:

> Norma Jean and Leroy were at the drive-in, watching a double feature (*Dr. Strangelove* and *Lover Come Back*), and the baby was sleeping in the back seat. When the first movie ended the baby was dead. It was the sudden infant death syndrome.
> . . . Leroy can hardly remember the child anymore, but he still sees vividly a scene from *Dr. Strangelove* in which the President of the United States was talking in a folksy voice on the hot line to the Soviet premier about the bomb accidentally headed towards Russia. He was in the War Room, and the world map was lit up. Leroy remembers Norma Jean standing catatonically beside him in the hospital and himself thinking: Who is this strange girl? He had forgotten who she was.[13]

Those unfamiliar with this style may be deterred by its apparent levity, and if this is satire then it is satire of the most savage order, because it would be parodying Leroy's apparently imbecilic inability to grieve his son. I would argue that the techniques on view here are not employed for satirical effect, however; Mason frequently writes in this way, concentrating on the surface details of a trauma and carefully avoiding anything that might lead the reader towards identifying a central character, or towards 'understanding' the character in the traditional fictional way. Diane Johnson's review of *In Country*, in which she refers to 'Shiloh', is surprisingly acute on the subject of Mason's *modus operandi*:

> But what does strike one as new has to do with [new American fiction writers'] method, in particular, of narrative distance. Most familiar is the sort of traditional novel as practiced by James or Bellow, in which you see through the eyes of the characters . . . now we could say that this is fiction of the 'other', in which the authors, very detached, describe mostly what can be seen, and the clarity of visual detail strangely objectifies the characters.[14]

In the passage above from 'Shiloh', Mason concentrates on what Leroy remembers rather than on what can be seen, but the effect is identical to Johnson's analysis; Leroy's memories are in effect 'visions', and the author does not provide any of the emotional baggage that presumably accompanies them. Johnson says of 'Shiloh':

> Neither Leroy nor Norma Jean seems to connect the emptiness of their lives with the loss of their baby, or boredom, or any of the things that brisk psychologist, the reader, supplies in explanation.[15]

Duncan Webster, in his book *Looka Yonder!* (subtitled 'The Imaginary American of Populist Culture'), points out that this is a 'fairly general experience of reading . . . the reader "knows" for example, that Jane Austen's Elizabeth and Darcy are in love and will marry well before the characters themselves do. . . .'[16] This is, I feel, only a partial explanation of the narrative distance operating in *Shiloh*, and why Diane Johnson's account of it is inadequate. I would argue that Leroy and Norma Jean have indeed connected their stagnant relationship (at the end of the story, Norma Jean announces to Leroy that she is leaving him, although typically there is no kind of resolution provided) with their loss, but they simply choose not to confront their awareness or attempt to articulate it.

There is an important indication of this when Norma Jean's mother Mabel tells her daughter of a gruesome incident in which a dachshund mauled a baby. Later, Norma Jean tries to discuss Mabel's motives with Leroy:

> 'She just said that about the baby because she caught me smoking. She's trying to pay me back.'
> 'What are you talking about?' Leroy says, nervously shuffling blueprints.
> 'You know good and well', Norma Jean says. . . . 'The very idea, her bringing up a subject like that! Saying it was neglect.'
> 'She didn't mean that,' Leroy says.[17]

This is their only discussion about their son in the story, and even then the child, or the subject of his death, is referred to by an indefinite pronoun. At the end of the conversation, Leroy pours Norma Jean a beer: 'For a long time they sit by the kitchen window watching the birds at the feeder.'[18] The scene ends.

Mason's narrative distance would thus appear to be connected with her characters' inability to face up to their lives; and the blankness of her prose, her focus on the surfaces of the couple's lives, is an attempt to recreate stylistically an absence or shortfall in the people themselves. This dovetailing of style and theme links her with writers such as Carver and Ford, despite differences in setting and approach.

The other major theme that Mason touches on in *Shiloh*, as I have mentioned, is the awkward readjustment of relationships between the sexes in the wake of the changes in the South: the decline of farming and its attendant community, the embourgeoisement of the young, the changing aspirations of women (although in Kentucky the latter takes a somewhat muted form). In the title story, Norma Jean lifts weights while her husband makes models from kits; in 'The Rookers', the second story in the collection, Mack struggles painfully through the books that he believes his daughter Judy is studying at college. (She is the first member of the family to benefit from a further education.) When she returns to visit her parents, Mack discovers that this self-improvement has been in vain: Judy has been studying physics while Mack has been reading up on philosophy. It is a poignant moment, as it seems to complete Mack's alienation from the womenfolk who constitute the rest of his family.

'The Rookers' is more explicit than much of Mason's work, and its final paragraph contains an eloquent summary of one of the strands of this first collection. Mack has been anxiously 'phoning a weather information service for news of an impending snowstorm, and the story ends there, with Mack in 'a frozen pose':

> Mary Lou suddenly realizes that Mack calls the temperature number because he is afraid to talk on the telephone, and by listening to a recording, he doesn't have to reply. It's his way of pretending he's involved. He wants it to snow so he won't have to go outside. He's afraid of what might happen. But it occurs to her that what he is really afraid of is women. Then Mary Lou feels so sick and heavy with her power over him that she wants to cry.[19]

These are echoes and variations of this in stories such as 'A New-Wave Format', in which Edwin feels unnerved not only by his girl-friend Sabrina's youth but by her one year of college education, or 'Still Life with Watermelon', where Louise's husband Tom has gone off to Texas to be a cowboy. This is a typically wry Masonic touch: Tom's gesture towards a vanishing Southern masculine culture is both extravagant (he leaves wearing a T-shirt which reads 'You better get in line now 'cause I get better-looking every day') and doomed (he returns after a few weeks having crashed his car on a flat, straight and deserted road north of Amarillo).

In an interview with the author in 1989 to coincide with the publication of her second volume of short stories, *Love Life*, Mason explained that

> the reason the men seemed weak in the stories in *Shiloh* is that the women were going through these changes that totally bewildered them, and that kind of incapacitated the men—especially in this kind of culture. It's agricultural, and the rôles are very clearly and strongly defined, very traditional. These rôles tend to break down later than they do in the cities, and when they do finally start to break down, the men are much more confused by the women than they would have been if they'd had more preparation.[20]

Mason used the character of Louise in 'Still Life with Watermelons' to illustrate how the stories in *Love Life* differ from those in the previous collection:

The main difference to me is that the world of the characters has changed, and they're further along in their relationships with the modern world. They're more sophisticated than they were when they started out. I find this an enormously rapid development in the culture, and I can no longer write about, say, Louise, or at least not Louise as she was. She'd be very different now.[21]

Louise (whose lack of sophistication is evinced, among other ways, by her passive response to her husband's eventual return) is not the only character in *Shiloh* that Mason would probably not attempt to write about now. Several other characters, Leroy and Norma Jean among them, would have undergone a series of changes during the course of the '80s, and it is instructive to examine the stories and people of *Love Life* in the light of the earlier collection.

The characters in *Love Life* may be, as Mason has said, 'further along in their relationships with the modern world', but that is not to imply that this shift has brought them any closer to absorbing the rearrangements in a way that fulfils them. The stories in the later collection are studded with failed relationships and confused people, just as the first volume was, but it is clear that these failures and confusions spring from a different stage in the modern history of the South.

A particularly interesting story in this respect is 'Airwaves', which features a depiction of what Mason calls 'the new Southern man'. Coy Wilson is certainly a contrast to the paralysed, feckless males of the earlier stories, and despite the fact that the story begins with him estranged from his girl-friend Jane because he could not allow her to support him through a period of unemployment, Jane thinks of him thus:

> He was appreciative of fine things most men wouldn't notice, such as flowers and pretty dishes. Coy was tender in his lovemaking, with more sensitivity than men were usually given credit for.[22]

Coy throws up a new set of problems unknown to the women of the *Shiloh* stories, however. Jane's description continues:

> On Phil Donahue's show, when the topic was sex, the women in the audience always said they wanted men who were gentle and considerate and involved in a lot of touching during the day instead of 'wham-bam-thank-you-mam' at the end of the day. Coy was the answer to those women's prayers, but he went too far. He was so fragile, with his nervous stomach. He couldn't watch meat being cut up. Jane still finds broken rolls of Tums stashed around the apartment.[23]

'Airwaves' can be read as an updated 'Shiloh': Jane's apparent decision to join the Army at the end of the story has the same kind of jokey assertiveness as Norma Jean's bodybuilding, and Coy's tenderness and sensitivity is a slightly healthier version of Leroy's model-making. The problem with this kind of reading is that it crudifies the story beyond all recognition, and it should be stressed that there are many other elements in 'Airwaves' which prevent such a straightforward satirical interpretation. The title, for example, refers to a recurring motif which begins with Jane's freedom to listen to a rock station that Coy disliked now he has moved out, and continues with her preacher brother's phoney ability to speak in tongues (Jane had imagined before seeing him in action it was 'an involuntary expression—a kind of gibberish that pours forth when people are possessed by the spirit of God'[24]). Her interest in the Army, therefore—she wants to sign up with 'Communications and Electronic Operations'—is as emblematic of her vague, half-understood desire to somehow 'tune herself in', as it were, as it is of a world in which sexual rôles have become confused.

Similarly, it would be easy to misinterpret Coy's nervous stomach and tender love-making as a parody of the New Man we have heard so much about in the last few years (and who at the time of writing is central to several advertising campaigns). This 'New Southern Man' is something slightly different; Mason has described Coy to the author as 'sensitive physically, but without much emotional depth'. She went on to explain that

> These guys in generations past, they were on the farm. Now they're kind of flipped into this whole new commercial venture where they have to wear a suit or a sport-coat, and

they have a title and a little bit of importance. And it's a false importance.

This is exactly Coy's situation: he eventually finds work as a floor-walker, supervising the girls at the tills in a large department store. After visiting him in the store, Jane reflects on his new job:

> Driving out of the parking lot, she thought how proudly Coy had said 'We're taking inventory', as though he were in thick with Wal-Mart executives. It didn't seem like him. She had deluded herself, expecting more of him just because he was such a sweet lover.[25]

As with all Mason's stories, attempts to extract one element from 'Airwaves' overbalances it and makes it sound clumsy. It would seem clear, however, that Coy's work, and his attitude to Jane, are as central to the story as Jane herself, and that Mason's concerns, in 'Airwaves' and elsewhere in *Love Life*, are to do with, in effect, folk memories: both Coy and Jane seem dimly aware that at some stage in the history of their native soil, things were different. These two are typical of the characters in the collection in that they belong to a different generation. Leroy and Norma Jean, and Mack and Mary Lou, can rely on their own rather than other people's memories to tell them how men and women have changed in their attitudes towards each other.

Although many of the relationships in *Love Life* are as messy and problematic (and yet undramatic) as that of Coy and Jane, the preceding story, 'Coyotes', differs because its central male character Cobb's obvious devotion to his fiancée Lynette compels him to readjust to her, even though this cause him confusion. The first paragraph of 'Coyotes' introduces Lynette as a recognizable Mason type:

> Cobb's fiancée, Lynette Johnson, wasn't interested in bridal magazines or china patterns or any of that girl stuff. Even when he brought up the subject of honeymoons she would joke about some impossible place—Bulgaria, Hong Kong, Lapland, Peru.[26]

Their planned wedding forms the basis of the story, although Mason approaches it with characteristic understatement, and the reader is given few clues as to the attitudes of Cobb, Lynette or, of course, given Mason's customary distance from her characters, the author. However, Cobb seems prepared to make a commitment to Lynette, despite her unconventionality and her apparent antipathy towards marriage; and although 'Coyotes' ends tentatively, with Cobb recognizing that this commitment may well be a mistake, his tolerance and clarity of thought is in contrast to the behaviour of several of the other men in the collection.

In 'Coyotes', Lynette works in a film-developing shop, and she tells Cobb and his family how she recently processed some photographs of a murder victim for the local sheriff:

> It was weird to see somebody's picture in the newspaper and then see the person all strung out on a table with bullet holes in his head, and still be able to recognise the person. The picture they ran was a school picture. That was really sad. School pictures are so embarrassing.[27]

It is a tiny moment in the story, and yet this technique, wherein the past comes perfectly preserved into the present, is commonly used in Mason's work: the past and its influence on the present is a key theme. I have already referred to the 'folk memories' that seem to influence the behaviour of Coy and Jane in 'Airwaves', but in Mason's novel *In Country* the author tackles the influence of the past more directly.

In Country is the story of 17-year-old Sam and her attempts in the summer of 1984 to understand her own family history; her father was killed in Vietnam just after her birth. To assist her in her search she has her uncle Emmett, a war veteran with whom she shares her mother's house near Paducah (her mother has remarried and left the area), veteran friends of Emmett, and her father's letters to her mother from the war, as well as her father's parents.

It is her father's letters which obviously provide the freshest route back to the past, but there are other echoes similar to Lynette's photographs—the rock music of the 1960s, for example. Sam is particularly fascinated by a 'new' Beatles song that she hears on the radio, an old R&B recording entitled 'Leave My Kitten Alone', hitherto unreleased, that the group made before they became famous. Mason's use of music throughout her stories is interesting, and I shall return to it later, but her inclusion of 'Leave My Kitten Alone' is especially effective since it allows Sam to hear an authentic slice of the '60s to which she has been previously unexposed.

> Rock-95 was playing that Beatles song again. She would recognise the Beatles anywhere. John was singing the lead. 'You better leave my kitten all alone,' he sang. 'I told you, big fat bulldog, you better leave her alone.' Sam had to find that record. She wanted to play it for everyone she loved. It was a fresh message from the past, something to go on.[28]

Sam will find more fresh messages from the past, but the Beatles record sets the tone for such discoveries, providing Sam with a way to form her own relationship with the Vietnam decade rather than the well-worn and familiar artefacts that the '60s and the war have spawned.

If the Beatles song is an important motif in the novel, the TV programme *M.A.S.H.* figures even more strongly, and the characters from the series—Trapper John, Radar, Hawkeye—become as familiar to the reader as some of Mason's own minor characters. Obviously the programme's Korean War setting allows Sam to make parallels with her father, but what is particularly interesting is Mason's own relationship with popular culture. Open any page of *In Country* and the reader will find the text peppered with italic references to films, pop music, TV shows; indeed, such is the obscurity of some of these references that one fears that Mason's work will need extensive footnotes long before that of any of her contemporaries.

The author herself has interesting observations on this aspect of her writing. 'It's not like these programmes and songs are just buzzing on in the background and the people aren't listening to them', she told the author in 1989.

> I think what writers typically do is throw these references in to make a comment on the culture, and the comment is always negative: popular culture is trash. I don't do that. I think I use the references more organically, to say, this is the world of the characters and this is what they like. The fact that the culture may be shallow doesn't mean that the characters are shallow, or that they are stupid for enjoying it.[29]

It is possible that much of Mason's reputation in some quarters as a satirist stems from the mistaken notion that she is indeed saying that popular culture *is* trash, and that her characters *are* stupid for enjoying it. The novelist and short-story writer Lorrie Moore, in her review of *Love Life*, describes aspects of the behaviour of some of Mason's characters and then goes on to say:

> If such living is morally hemmed in, strewn with the junk of our culture, it is all that Ms. Mason's characters can avail themselves of. Buried in the very gut of America, feeling deeply the lock and cage of the land, they send up antennae and receive what they are able to, what there is. If they are mocked and demeaned by what they consume, they do not know it: to mock and demean are coastal pastimes, of which they haven't the means to partake.[30]

Moore's review is otherwise sensitive and sympathetic to Mason's work, but she seems here to fail to understand the attitude of Mason's characters towards this culture. Certainly Sam understands it better than many critics of Mason's work would have us believe; the fact that she is an avid consumer of 'junk culture' does not prevent her from making critical judgements of it:

> On *M.A.S.H.* sometimes, things were too simple. She could see right through them. The night before, Dr. Sidney Freeman, the Army psychiatrist, arrived to treat Hawkeye's mysterious sneezing fits, and within ten minutes he had located the cause in a repressed childhood memory.[31]

Certainly Mason uses popular culture to comment on the moods and inner life of her characters, and occasionally this is done ironically, but there would appear to be more of an interaction than Moore would allow.

Duncan Webster has perceived another use of these references. In his analysis of Diane Johnson's review of *In Country* he points out that

> as soon as one notices that Bobbie Ann Mason's characters have Talking Heads tapes on their Walkmans or Springsteen on the car radio, an image of rural charm will no longer serve to characterize the novel.[32]

It is Mason's ability to portray the coexistence of a variety of cultures in *In Country* that characterizes the book (Webster argues that 'it's a novel about culture as much as it's about the war'). Two of these cultures are the culture of the 1980s and the culture of the 1960s, and the book seems to me entirely successful in its depiction of how these two cultures trade off each other. Diane Johnson's assertion that *In Country* is 'a Reaganesque dream novel', and that 'in the present . . . nothing bad can happen'[33] seems to be a careless attempt to support her image of the book as pastoral. (To Johnson, '*In Country* seems less a work of fearless realism than one of romantic pastoral charm in a tradition which includes, among other books, *Little Women*.') Emmett's inability to cope with contemporary America after his experiences in Vietnam contradicts this, but a more precise symbol of the past's influence on the present (and a further example of the way the past can reach the present in a perfectly preserved form) is his skin problem, which Sam fears may be as a result of exposure to Agent Orange. In the world of Mason's novel, his disease would appear to suggest precisely the opposite of what Johnson is trying to say: in the present, bad things can happen as a direct result of the bad things that have happened before.

In Country, Mason's most complete work, is a book of deceptive complexity. The techniques familiar from her short fiction—the distance of the author from her characters, the laconic presentation of trauma—serve to create a mood and style unique in modern American fiction, and Mason's refusal to resolve any of the narrative threads that emerge in the book is an interesting variant to the commonly accepted notions of what constitutes realism in fiction. (Emmett's skin disease is left undiagnosed, and his relationship with his girl-friend Anita is apparently motionless. Tom, a veteran friend of Emmett's with whom Sam becomes involved, has found no cure to the impotency that has plagued him since the war.) A critic has referred to 'the minute shifts of consciousness'[34] that characterize Mason's short fiction; *In Country* ends with an emotional visit by Emmett, Sam and her father's mother to the Washington Memorial (one of the few occasions in any of Mason's writing that the action moves outside Kentucky), but in the world of the novel such a gesture is almost rhetorical: the characters can make peace with their history in this way, but no such truce is available with their current lives.

Spence + Lila, Mason's other major piece of writing, is disappointingly unambitious by comparison. That is not to say that its subject-matter is unimportant: Lila, wife of Spence and mother of Nancy and Cat, has to face the prospect of a mastectomy. Nancy Culpepper has appeared in two previous Mason stories, both in the *Shiloh* collection ('Nancy Culpepper' and 'Lying Doggo') and Mason has said that the Culpepper family is to a large extent autobiographical. Nancy is interesting in the light of an interview with Mason in *Granta 15*; talking about Nabokov (of whom Mason has written a study), she said:

> In some ways, comparing myself to him is like comparing Willie Nelson to an opera singer, but I felt connected to him because he had the sensibility of an exile, was working with two opposing cultures which made him peculiar, the same way I felt myself.[35]

In many ways, Mason is overstating her case here, of course; after all, many Americans move from one part of the country to another without necessarily feeling that they are émigrés. And Mason's assertion that she is working with two opposing cultures is to some extent questionable, in that this process is apparently an internal one, with its contradictions seemingly resolved by the time the reader approaches the finished product. Nancy, however, must work with two opposing cultures within *Spence + Lila*; her sense of dislocation which springs from returning home to Kentucky from the North to be with her mother is discernible, though, of course, understated.

Spence + Lila, though recognizably the product of the author of *In Country* and the short fiction, seems the least successful of all Mason's work, and despite its interestingly distanced approach to Lila's cancer (the book may be autobiographical, but Mason's ability to approach the illness without emotional baggage is surprisingly reminiscent of Emmett's Agent Orange and Leroy's impressionistic memories of the loss of his son), it is possible that Mason's closeness to the material does not suit her. Its essential domesticity fails to resonate in the way that similar scenes elsewhere in her fiction do, possibly because the contradictions and tensions of the novella lie on its surface in the narrative, rather than unspoken in the lives and minds of the characters.

Bobbie Ann Mason's contribution to current American literature is as yet slight, and until the body of her work has swelled a little it is hard to regard her in the same light as a Richard Ford or an Anne Tyler. The issues that her writing raises, however, and the critical responses to her work so far, are central to important and long-standing arguments about regionalist writing, as we have seen. But her writing also relates to another more contemporary debate currently raging in U.S. literary circles, a debate prompted by Tom Wolfe. Wolfe has been arguing since the 1960s that Balzac has set the model for fiction, that novelists have some kind of responsibility as the standard-bearers of social realism, and fabulists such as John Barth, or modernists such as Thomas Pynchon, are somehow abnegating their duties by looking internally rather than externally. In the '60s this argument had a certain potency: there was little fictional realism, and Tom Wolfe and his fellow New Journalists consequently hijacked fictional techniques and used them in a number of fascinating magazine features.

Mason has acknowledged that Wolfe's arguments may well have influenced her and others to seize back Balzac's legacy:

> [Wolfe] said that fiction writers just weren't looking at what was happening in the world, they were befuddled by it. So they turned their backs on it and started writing all these phantasmagoric, surrealist things, experimental things. So maybe our trend towards realism was a breaking away from all that.[36]

The irony here is that while Wolfe's original argument (in his introduction to *The New Journalism*) seems to have provoked an outpouring of American realist writing, Wolfe has repeated his assertions very recently, as if unaware of the existence of many of the writers discussed in this volume. His renewed attack on American writers must be taken with a pinch of salt, as it would appear to be part of a publicity campaign for his own novel *The Bonfire of the Vanities*, and by implication he is proclaiming himself as the only contemporary American heir to Balzac's realist throne. However, the fact that regionalist writers like Mason seem so little understood, and that her work in particular continues to be discussed in terms that preclude adequate critical analysis, suggest that her close scrutiny of the changes in contemporary American society may well go ignored. Mason may not be Balzac, but there is no one in America who corresponds quite as closely to Wolfe's notions of what constitutes a fiction writer.

NOTES

1. Stephen Amidon, *Literary Review*, December 1989.
2. Barbara Trapido, *Sunday Times*, 24 November 1989.
3. Robert Nye, *Weekend Guardian*, 25 November 1989.
4. Flannery O'Connor, *Everything that Rises Must Converge* (Faber, 1980), p. vii.
5. Quoted in Duncan Webster, *Looka Yonder!* (Commedia/Routledge, 1988), p. 57.
6. Quoted in Webster, p. 47.
7. *New York Times Review of Books*, 7 November 1985.
8. Ibid.
9. *New York Times Book Review*, 26 November 1989.
10. Bobbie Ann Mason, *Shiloh* (Chatto and Windus, 1983), p. 1.
11. Ibid., p. 2.
12. Ibid., p. 1.
13. Ibid., pp. 4–5.
14. *New York Times Review of Books*, 7 November 1985.
15. Ibid.
16. Webster, p. 126.
17. Mason, *Shiloh*, p. 10.
18. Ibid., p. 10.
19. Ibid., p. 33.
20. Interview with the author, 1989 (a shorter version of the interview can be found in the *Daily Telegraph*, 4 December 1989).
21. Interview with the author, 1989.
22. Bobbie Ann Mason, *Love Life* (Chatto and Windus, 1989), p. 182.
23. Ibid., p. 182.
24. Interview with the author, 1989.
25. Mason, *Love Life*, p. 195.

26. Ibid., p. 161.
27. Ibid., p. 174.
28. Bobbie Ann Mason, *In Country* (Flamingo, 1987), p. 125.
29. *Daily Telegraph*, 4 December 1989.
30. *New York Times Book Review*, 26 November 1989.
31. Mason, *In Country*, p. 83.
32. Webster, *Looka Yonder!*, p. 127.
33. *New York Times Review of Books*, 7 November 1985.
34. Stephen Amidon, *Literary Review*, December 1989.
35. Quoted in Webster, *Looka Yonder!*, pp. 133–34.
36. *Daily Telegraph*, 4 December 1989.

5
Richard Ford

Of the dozen or so writers introduced to U.K. readers via *Granta*'s two anthologies of new American writing, *Dirty Realism* and *More Dirt*, Richard Ford is the one who has fulfilled all early promise and now deserves consideration as a major post-war American writer.

Ford's first novel, *A Piece of My Heart*, was published in the U.S. in 1976, but it remained unavailable in Britain until 1987, when interest in Ford had been considerably heightened by the publication here of his 1986 novel *The Sportswriter*, his third book. British readers, as we shall see, thus received a very different introduction to Ford's style.

Richard Ford's background, and his close friendship with Raymond Carver (possibly the central figure that binds together many of the writers dealt with in this book), have been well documented, but are worth repeating here. Ford was born in Mississippi—he grew up very near the house where Eudora Welty spent her childhood—and if there is such a thing as a 'dirty realist' (although this has become an inadequate categorization for these writers), then Ford can lay better claim to the term than most. His mother was born in a dirt cabin in Arkansas (as was Carver's), and he trained both as a marine and as a boxer. He has never tried to use these credentials to foster an image of dirt-poor country boy made good: 'People do say how come, when you've lived such a sweet life yourself, you can write about people whose lives are not so sweet?' he once remarked.[1] Like Carver, though, his upbringing was resolutely unliterary (he has said that his reading matter consisted of Mickey Spillane thrillers, Zane Grey westerns, the Bible and a range of sports magazines) and for the most part his characters, like the characters in much of contemporary American fiction, do not themselves have much use for books.

A Piece of My Heart is set on an island in the Mississippi, and predictably critics, particularly English critics, reached immediately for their Southern writers pack. Bernard Levin in the *Sunday Times* mentions Faulkner, Tennessee Williams and 'that man who wrote *Tobacco Road*'[2]; Lorna Sage in the *Observer* is reminded of Flannery O'Connor.[3] (If P. G. Wodehouse had decided to place Blandings Castle in Arkansas, no doubt he too would have been compared to O'Connor.)

Sam Newel and Robard Hewes, two men with very different backgrounds and with no prior connection, have both come to the island to hide away temporarily. Hewes has taken a job assisting Mr. Lamb, the island's owner (and without wishing to squeeze Ford uncomfortably into any tradition, Lamb is the kind of Southern grotesque that literary critics would seize upon), so that he can renew an adulterous relationship with his cousin Beuna, who lives nearby; Newel, a trainee lawyer, has come down from Chicago in an attempt to rid himself of the indecisions and lack of direction that have been plaguing his life. The novel is divided into sections that deal with each man in turn, but it begins memorably with a short flash-forward prologue in which W. W. (Beuna's husband), pursuing Hewes, comes across a youth holding a gun:

> 'I come after Robard Hewes. I guess you hadn' seen him.'
> 'Come who?'
> 'Robard Hewes.'
> 'Well, W. W.,' the boy said, flicking the corners of his mouth with his tongue and letting the tip of his rifle sink back to his foot, 'I never did hear of him. But I'll tell you one thing.'
> 'And what's that?'' W. W. said.
> 'I just did kill a man here, wasn't a minute past you driving up.'[4]

The reader's awareness of Robard's death inevitably invests the tale with a greater tension (and indeed any flaw in the novel stems from the fact that Hewes's story, dealing as it does with a man obsessed by lust, is more compulsive than Newel's existential quest). But the prologue serves an important function in setting a tone, for in *A Piece of My Heart*, not only is life cheap, but its end frequently lacks dignity or even solemnity. The father of Newel's girl-friend Beebe died, we are told, when he attempted to drown himself in the river; his leap off the bridge, however, only takes him onto the concrete piling below. Hewes's father drowned inside his car during a flash flood; Newel's father, a travelling salesman, was decapitated in his car by corrugated steel piping. ('Left him sitting in the front seat. He could've kept on driving if he'd had a head.'[5]) In one of the novel's most celebrated scenes, Lamb, the almost Dickensian owner of the island, dies when he electrocutes himself with the ancient gadget he uses to stun fish. (' "Oops," the old man said in obvious surprise, and threw up both his hands. . . .'[6])

The mood invoked by these freakish deaths is reinforced by vivid descriptions of the grisly ends of a variety of animals: Newel remembers a friend blasting an owl to pieces with a shot-gun, and when Newel and Hewes are being taken over to the island they watch a deer attempting to cross the river being dragged underwater by a crocodile. Early on in the novel, when Hewes has to stay at a little motel, he finds a jack rabbit shivering in a bobcat's cage; the bobcat is waiting for the evening cool to arrive before he eats his supper (much as the reader is waiting for the end of the novel to find out precisely how Hewes meets his end). It is impossible to imagine a world more different from the suburban calm of *The Sportswriter*.

When asked about the 'fearfulness' of the book, Ford replied:

> To say true, that was the way I was feeling about myself when I wrote it. I wrote it in Michigan where I had a feeling of utter displacement. I had a grant and I had . . . no excuses not to write it, and I felt fearful. It's a book about displacement, about trying to discriminate between love and sex, about trying to stay alive.[7]

This explanation is somewhat melodramatic; the equation of the author's mental state during the creation of his novel with the desperate lives of the book's characters is almost comically overstrained. And yet one of Ford's skills as a writer is to find frameworks in which he can portray the most mundane, and yet the most crucial, feelings and attitudes and ideas, without the use of characters who can necessarily articulate the complexities of their situations.

The concerns of the book that Ford isolates above—displacement, love and sex, survival—sound bland when removed from the extraordinarily atmospheric setting that Ford gives them in *A Piece of My Heart*, but in the context of the book their implications are brought into riveting focus. It should be pointed out that there is a notable mordant wit at work here (Ford is rarely given credit for being funny, and yet when he reads his own work he is careful to bring out the wry humour of his writing): the absurd sexual tension between Hewes and Beuna in particular reaches an exaggerated pitch which serves both to emphasize the power of their relationship and to allow a little light into the bleakness of the world of the novel. Beuna's apparent ability to achieve orgasm during a simple telephone conversation with Hewes, and her unorthodox way of scenting her letters to him, are glorious illustrations of a desire without any spiritual or romantic dimension.

As far as survival is concerned, Newel is one of the very few to make it through the book unscathed, possibly, due to his lack of active involvement in most aspects of his life. Towards the end of the novel, Newel explains to Hewes the reason for his visit to the island:

> 'I was going nuts up there trying to figure out if that jumble amounted to enough to say I ought to go back and pick it up again.'
> 'You like Chicago better now, do you?'
> 'I don't care,' he said.
> 'You come all the way down here and you're going back without having done nothin?'
> ... 'I figured one thing out,' he said ... 'I don't give a shit anymore....'[8]

Hewes, on the other hand, feels that 'as far as I'm concerned, things just happen. One minute don't learn the next one nothin.'[9] It is these delicate differences between them—Robard's involvement (with Beuna) and his reactive nature, Newel's lack of engagement and his inability to care—that ensures the death of one man and the continued existence of the other. *A Piece of My Heart* may not be as black as it has been painted, but there is still a grim nihilism at work here.

Ford's second novel, *The Ultimate Good Luck*, only intensifies the darkness. Ford himself has called it 'a brutal little book without much light shining through it', and despite its superficial resemblances to his début (the powerful sense of place—a small, shabby town in Mexico—and of dislocation), it remains the least successful book in the Ford *corpus*, a Spillane thriller with metaphysical pretensions, and the writer will return to its theme—the nature of luck—with more success later in his career. It is the third book, *The Sportswriter*, that marks Ford out as a major contemporary American novelist.

According to Ford, *The Sportswriter* was written at the suggestion of his wife, who asked him why he did not write about people who were happy. It says much for Ford's world-view that what he then produced was a novel seen variously as being about 'depression',[10] 'a mid-life crisis'[11] and 'a weekend in hell'.[12]

Certainly it is in parts a painful book, but this is not necessarily at odds with the 'brief' that Ford was given by his wife; *The Sportswriter* is in effect the study of one man's attempt to live a life that is optimistic and good-humoured, despite its traumas. The first-person narrative that Ford uses for the book is wonderfully gauged, reminiscent in its bluff, cheery matter-of-factness of the voice in Walker Percy's 1961 novel *The Moviegoer*, and perhaps Ford's title is a deliberate echo.

The book is an account of the Easter weekend of Frank Bascombe, the sports-writer of the title. Bascombe is in his late thirties, and came to his present job after a brief but apparently promising career as a fiction-writer: his book of short stories received favourable reviews and was optioned by a Hollywood producer. Bascombe is recently divorced from a wife who is referred to only as 'X' throughout the book. (According to Ford, he left 'X' in the manuscript because he could not think of a name he was happy with; eventually he left her anonymous because Bascombe 'could not say her name, that what had happened between them made her name just not sayable'.[13] It is an intriguing idea, but one that sits a little uneasily with other notions of the central character that present themselves throughout the novel.)

The reasons for their divorce are complex. The separation itself was occasioned by X's discovery of some letters to Frank from a woman; in fact, there was no affair, and the letters are entirely innocent, but Frank's refusal to comfort his wife leads her to believe otherwise. X's parents, with whom Frank has kept in contact, believe that their estrangement was caused by the shattering death (from Raye's syndrome) of their eldest son Ralph, but Frank is unsure whether this is the case. Frank prefers to blame events on his 'dreaminess';

> Sometimes I would wake up in the morning and open my eyes to X lying beside me breathing, and not recognize her! Not even know what town I was in, or how old I was, or what life it was, so dense was I in my particular dreaminess. I would lie there and try as best I could to extend not knowing, feel that pleasant soaring-out-of-azimuth-and-attitude sensation I grew to like as long as it would last, while twenty possibilities for who, where, what went by. . . . I know you can dream your way through an otherwise fine life, and never wake up, which is what I almost did. I believe I have survived that now and put dreaminess behind me. . . .[14]

This passage touches on two of Bascombe's most cherished philosophies: that dreaminess is dangerous ('one should avoid it if you're lucky enough to know it exists'[15]) and that choice is a crucial method of survival:

> A woman . . . once told me that I had too many choices, that I was not driven enough by dire necessity. But that is just an illusion and her mistake. Choices are what we all need.[16]

Frank's almost formulaic *modus vivendi*, which ensures a life which he at least can come to regard as a happy one, is complex. It involves a number of key principles, and these principles are repeated enthusiastically throughout the novel, as if Bascombe is trying to convince himself of their efficacy.

'In that book', said Ford of *The Sportswriter* in 1989, 'I tried to resurrect a mystery from facts.'[17] On the face of it these words have only an antithetical relationship, but Bascombe insists that 'literalism' and 'mystery'—both, in his view, necessary qualities in a life—can in fact be complementary. Bascombe lives in Haddam, New Jersey 'because it is not a hard town to understand':

> ... a small-town, out-of-the-mainstream feeling exists here, as engrossed as any in New Hampshire, but retaining the best of what New Jersey offers: assurance that mystery is never longed for, nor meaningful mystery shunned.[18]

Haddam, then, is a place 'where it is not at all hard for a literalist to contemplate the world'[19]; it is 'as straightforward and plumb-literal as a fire hydrant, which more than anything else makes it the pleasant place it is'.[20] Frank's girl-friend Vicki, an uncomplicated Texan, is, says Frank approvingly, 'in no part a dreamer, I know it, but a literalist from the word go, happy to let the world please her in the small ways it can'.[21] Occasionally Ford has fun with Bascombe's obsession with plainness; when asked by an interviewee about his taste in art, Frank professes a fondness for the work of Winslow Homer: 'He'd paint Walled Lake here, and it'd feel and look pretty much like this, I guess.'[22]

These twin pillars of literalism and mystery are frequently linked in the text. Bascombe's obsession with catalogues after the death of his son springs from the world they depict being 'knowable, safe-and-sound. Everybody with exactly what they need or could get. A perfect illustration of how the literal can become the mildly mysterious.'[23] An old girl-friend 'gave in to the literal in life and almost nothing else, and for that reason mystery emanated from her like a fire-alarm'.[24] Even Bascombe's job fits neatly into his world-view: 'athletes at the height of their powers make literalness into a mystery all of its own simply by becoming absorbed in what they're doing.'[25] Indeed, it is when Bascombe describes his fascination with sportsmen that he provides his most succinct self-portrait:

> . . . years of athletics training teach this; the necessity of relinquishing doubt and ambiguity and self-inquiry in favor of a pleasant, self-championing one-dimensionality which has instant rewards in sports.[26]

And, apparently, in the world outside the arena; Bascombe's 'pleasant, self-championing one-dimensionality' seems to have brought him all the rewards that he needs.

Whereas literalism is an essential tool for survival, factualism is, in Bascombe's eyes, an altogether different and in no way laudatory science. If literalists are happy to view the world as it is, refuse to delve beneath its surface, and allow mystery to emanate from this blank acceptance, factualists are reductionists, determined to break the world into digestible chunks. Bascombe is unhappy that X no longer forces Paul and Clarissa, his two surviving children, to attend church,

> not because they will turn out godless (I couldn't care less) but because she is bringing them up to be perfect little factualists and information accumulators with no particular reverence or speculative interest for what's not known. . . . You can, after all, know too damn much and end up with a big thumping loss you can't replenish.[27]

Bascombe's complicated and ingenious philosophy has two further supporting principles: firstly,

> that for your life to be worth anything, you must sooner or later face down the possibility of terrible, searing regret. Though you must also manage to avoid it or your life will be ruined.[28]

—and secondly, that

> all we really want is to get to the point where the past can explain nothing about us and we can get on with life. Whose history can ever reveal very much?[29]

Robard Hewes in *A Piece of My Heart* expressed as much with his dictum that 'One minute don't teach the next one nothin'; the voice may have changed, but the ideas remain much the same.

Avoiding regret is something that Bascombe claims to have succeeded in doing. The central problem that Ford poses for himself in *The Sportswriter* is to convince the reader that a man who has experienced the death of his child and the end of a marriage has achieved equanimity without some form of psychic damage; the reactions to the book quoted earlier suggest that many readers and critics were resistant to the idea. Yet on the evidence of the text, Bascombe is indeed a happy man. His conviction that history is bunk, of course, is linked to his attitude to regret (which necessitates a contemplation of the past). Thus when he does come to articulate his recent traumas, the language he uses is correspondingly muted: 'I would not change much, if anything at all', he tells us in the first chapter. 'I might not choose to get divorced. And my son . . . would not die. But that's about it for these matters.'[30] This kind of shoulder-shrugging acceptance of tragedy may show that Bascombe has indeed accepted his lot, that he has managed to avoid regret and thus ruin, but it carries within it a strangeness that prevents our identification; Bascombe occasionally appears as alienated and as dislocated as the hero of Camus' *L'Étranger*.

It is in his relationships that this dislocation is most obvious. His speculations on the likely course of future relationships with people he hardly knows possess a dreaminess of the kind he is convinced he has excised; at Vicki's parents' house, Bascombe finds himself hoping that

> her dad and I could become bosom buddies even if Vicki and I didn't work things out. He and I could still be friends. If his tire went flat some rainy night in Haddam or Hightstown or any place within my area code, he could call me up, I'd drive out to get him . . . he would go off into the Jersey darkness certain he had a friend worthy of his trust.[31]

That Frank has not yet even met Vicki's father is of no import; the point is that the possibilities are there ('options are what we all need'). Frank's sexual exploits in the last two years of his marriage ('I must've slept with eighteen women—a number I don't consider high, or especially scandalous or surprising under the circumstances'[32]) sprang not from any Lothario-like quality in his nature, but from a similar sort of dreaminess to the one that marks his desire for a friendship with Wade, Vicki's father. 'All at once I was longing for all my worth to be a part of that life,' he says, contemplating these women,

> longing to enter completely into that little existence of hers as a full (if brief) participant, share her secret illusions, hopes. 'I love you,' I've heard myself say more than once to a Becky, Sharon, Susie or Marge I hadn't known longer than *four hours and fifteen minutes*.[33]

His relationship with Vicki may be monogamous, but it is hardly satisfactory (and ends with Vicki delivering a mighty punch to the jaw, rarely an indication of harmony). Yet typically Frank has managed to construct a *modus vivendi* in this relationship, as he has with the rest of his life; equally typically, it is based on omissions ('Our own talk is always of the jokey-quippy-irony style and lets us leap happily over "certain things" to other "certain things"—cozy intimacy, sex and rapture. . .'[34]), and thus Vicki fits snugly into Frank's world, with its strict boundaries beyond which nothing is contemplated. At the disastrous lunch with Vicki's parent's, Frank launches into a long and trite hymn to team spirit; when he comes to the end, he knows that the atmosphere between him and Vicki has changed:

> There is trouble, as I've suspected, on the horizon. I have talked too much to suit her and, worse, said the wrong things. . . . This may have amounted to a betrayal, an illusion torn, causing doubt to bloom into dislike.[35]

Yet this realization (shortly confirmed by the punch) does not prevent him from asking Vicki to marry him: his dreaminess is such that he seems genuinely able to imagine a life for them together ('a life of small flourishes and clean napkins'[36]), just as he is able to imagine a repaired relationship with X on the way to Detroit with Vicki.

There are two key events in the novel that test Bascombe's ideas, events which smack of despair and panic and depression and which Frank must keep at arm's length in order to survive. The first is his interview with Herb Wallagher, an ex-football player now confined to a wheel-chair. Frank's angle on Herb ('who has become an inspiration to his former teammates by demonstrating courage and determination, going back to college, finishing his degree in communication arts, marrying his black physiotherapist. . .'[37]) will be 'Make a Contribution': 'It is the kind of story I enjoy and find easy to write.'[38]

The interview, however, is a disaster: Herb has obviously been unable to 'make a contribution', and seems deep in the throes of a manic depression. His face dotted with toilet paper from shaving cuts, he bursts into tears, confides that his neighbours still think he plays on the team, and answers Frank's questions with a blunt 'You're an asshole.'[39] It is a blackly comic episode, yet it provides both Bascombe and the reader with a terrifying glimpse of what lies just beyond the sports-writer's perimeters (he is, predictably, unable to write up the story).

The second, more substantial test of Frank's equilibrium is the suicide of Walter, a co-member of the Divorced Men's Club, who has recently confessed to Bascombe that he had a one-night stand with a man in a New York hotel. Frank does not want to hear the confession, nor does he want any kind of relationship with Walter; the characters and survival mechanisms of the two men are wildly dissimilar. It is Walter's suicide that serves to persuade the reader that Bascombe's exclusion of more or less everything that we commonly regard as human experience may have something to commend itself. Walter simply does not possess Frank's resources, as Frank explains to X when they visit Walter's house after the suicide:

> Walter gave himself up to the here and now, but he got stranded. Then I think he got excited, and all he knew how to do was sentimentalize his life, which made him regret everything. If he'd made it past today he'd have been fine, I think.[40]

Frank responds to Herb by refusing to write up the story as he knows it to be; in Walter's house (and Frank has come straight from Vicki's parents) he suggests to X that they should climb into the dead man's bed and make love, a suggestion that understandably appals X.

Walter's death does provoke something of a crisis in Frank (a typically muted one), and he finds himself taking a train to

New York. He is rescued, once again, by a woman, a young college girl gaining some work experience at the magazine, whose presence is seized upon by Bascombe:

> I hear her feet skip-skip down the carpeted corridor, hear the door to the ladies' sigh open, sigh back, bump shut. . . . And there is no nicer time on earth than now—everything in the offing, nothing going wrong, all potential. . . . This is really all life is worth, when you come down to it.[41]

Whether the girl's emergence is necessarily fortuitous is debatable; Frank Bascombe's charm and decency ensures that there will always be a Vicki or a Catherine along to rescue him, and he can immerse himself temporarily and happily in another life, but temporary immersion is a questionable solution to the question of how to conduct one's life.

In the novel's coda, Frank finds himself living in Florida almost by accident, and Florida makes perfect sense both for and to him:

> Coming to the bottom of the country provokes a nice sensation, a tropical certainty that something will happen to you here. The whole place seems alive with modest hopes. People in Florida, I've discovered, are here to get away from things, to seek no end of life, and there is a crispness and a rightness to everyone's life that I find likable.[42]

The Sportswriter was written right in the middle of the Reagan years. It would be fatuous to over-emphasize the book's political content or meaning; politics is only touched upon twice, very briefly. The first time is during a conversation that Frank conducts with a liberal neighbour over the garden fence, when she expresses her concern about U.S. foreign policy in Latin America: 'I've been out of town a couple of days, Dee', Frank replies.[43] The second time is during lunch with Vicki's parents, when he confesses that he has not 'paid much attention to politics the last few years'.[44] And yet these statements seem entirely consistent with the image we now have of the Reagan years, and the absence of a political dimension is in a way an indicator of the political climate of the time. Certainly it is hard to imagine a Frank

Bascombe functioning quite so blithely in the Watergate mid-'70s or the Vietnam mid-'60s. It is possible that Ford has constructed a character who, in his inability to confront anything painful without first reducing it to manageable proportions, is the perfect inhabitant of a country which has spent ten years trying to feel good about itself. During the conversation with his neighbour, Frank finds that he

> cannot bring up the name or the face of the man who is president, and instead I see, unaccountably, the actor Richard Chamberlain wearing a burnoose and a nicely trimmed Edwardian beard.[45]

This is as close as Bascombe will come to a cogent political statement: of all the fiction discussed in this book, *The Sportswriter* comes closest to fulfilling Diane Johnson's description of Bobbie Ann Mason's *In Country* as 'a Reaganesque dream novel, where in the present nothing bad happens'.[46]

The Sportswriter remains the most important of Ford's books, and arguably one of the most important American novels of the last ten years, particularly in its embodiment of a national *Zeitgeist*. Bascombe is as memorable and as complex a character as Holden Caulfield or Percy's Jack Bolling, and the voice that Ford has found for him is as distinctive as any in post-war American fiction.

Ford followed *The Sportswriter* with a collection of short stories (*Rock Springs*, 1988) and a novella (*Wildlife*, 1990): the novella and stories are all set in or around Great Falls, Montana. 'I'm gonna write stories about Great Falls until I run it into the ground', he told Robert Winder in 1989.[47]

Ford's move to Montana was crucial too in helping him to find a voice which suits the concerns of the stories in *Rock Springs*, and the landscape of the mid-west is an overpowering presence; but the new dimension that Ford finds does not seem to spring wholly from geography. The novella and four of the best stories in *Rock Springs*—'Optimists', 'Children', 'Communist' and 'Great Falls'—all use a technique that has become a Ford trademark. It is a simple device: Ford uses a first-person narrative, and the narrator then looks back on a formative teenage experience with the benefit of an adult's hindsight. (These five pieces of fiction are all set in the years 1959–61; for what it is worth, the ages of the narrators correspond exactly with Ford's own age in those years—he was born in 1944—although the author has denied that they are in any way autobiographical:

> If you make up a whole new set of fictive features for a time in your own life that you lived through and which was very vivid . . . if you turn your attention away from yourself and towards something that you make up, there's a nice *torque*

Ford explained to the author in 1990.[48])

Frequently the openings of each story contain a summary of the narrative events that are about to unfold. Thus the first sentence of *Wildlife* is as follows:

> In the fall of 1960, when I was sixteen and my father was for a time not working, my mother met a man named Warren Miller and fell in love with him.[49]

Wildlife is about a great deal more than this, but its central incident is summarized in its first line. 'Optimists' similarly synopsizes the considerable drama of its few pages into its opening:

> All of this that I am about to tell happened when I was only fifteen years old, in 1959, the year my parents were divorced, the year when my father killed a man and went to prison for it. . . .[50]

The effect of this foreshadowing allows for a gentler, more contemplative tone, as it extracts some of the urgency from the narrative, and allows Ford to use the wistful, wise voice that we first heard in *The Sportswriter* (although none of the narrators in the 'teenage' stories possess Bascombe's complexity or his eerie calm). The hindsight that the narrators are given has allowed them to recognize the pivotal nature of the events they describe.

'Optimists' is typical both in this respect and in its fascination with the nature of luck, a theme that Ford first contemplated in his second novel. Its central event is the murder referred to in the opening sentence; but the nature of the killing, its bizarreness and terrifying suddenness, is crucial to the prevailing idea that chance is the single most important force in a life. The narrator's father Roy, a staunch union man, comes back from his job at the railroad and describes to his son Frank, his wife and his wife's guests how he has seen a man killed in an accident. He is highly disturbed by what he has witnessed, but the male guest, Boyd Mitchell, is highly critical both of Roy's failure to save the man and of the 'featherbedding practices of the union'. He provokes the other man to the extent that Roy punches him hard in the chest and kills him. It is a killing that was unimaginable even ten minutes before, and has no reference to anything that has happened between the two men in the past.

The consequences are predictably catastrophic: what is given particular emphasis is the way the family—mother, father, son—immediately disperse. Roy is in prison, Frank joins the army, the mother obtains a divorce and drifts away, losing touch with both of them. Thus three people who formed an apparently indivisible unit find, through an event of a freakish nature, that their connection has been loosed and that they have no further use for each other. It is stressed that the death is not the direct cause of the break-up (just as Frank Bascombe believes that his divorce was not caused by the death of his son); in fact the couple separate for reasons that seem arbitrary:

> But when he came out and went back on the railroad as a switchman the two of them argued about things, about her wanting us to go some place else to live—California or Seattle were mentioned. And then they separated, and she moved out.[51]

So it is not that the mother leaves the father because he has killed a man; it is that the murder has changed the pattern of their lives. Luck, in other words, dissolves what might otherwise have been indissoluble human bonds, and at the end of the story, when the adult Frank runs into his mother in a grocery store, it is the first time he has seen her for many years, and their conversation is tender and awkward. Neither of them has kept in touch with Roy. (Ford, incidentally, has described the conclusion as 'upbeat, even though I'm the only person in the world who thinks so'[52]; for the creator of

Frank Bascombe, these moments of tenderness are cause for celebration.)

There are literally scores of broken marriages to be found in *Rock Springs*. In both 'Sweethearts' and the title story, the narrator and his current wife have been married before; in 'Empire', Marge and her second husband Sims are travelling to see Marge's sister Pauline, who was a teacher in Seattle 'three husbands back'.[53] In two of the teenage stories, 'Optimists' and 'Great Falls', the narrative recounts how the parental marriage fell apart (and in 'Optimists' Frank refers to his own ex-wife). Given how luck, the ungovernable banality in the world of Ford's characters, can switch their lives around, it is perhaps hardly surprising that relationships should be such a frequent casualty, but it means that the kind of love experienced is of a highly transient nature. Russ, the narrator of 'Sweethearts', gives a succinct and atypically direct summation of his understanding of love:

> I knew what love was about. It was about not giving trouble nor inviting it. It was about not leaving a woman for the thought of another one. It was about never being in that place you said you'd never be in. And it was not about being alone. Never that. Never that.[54]

This is a variety of love that can accommodate several different partners during the course of a lifetime (and Russ's reference to 'the thought of' a new partner lends the statement an ambiguity which would be cleared by the omission of those three words. It would appear that this is more a warning against Bascombe-like dreaminess than it is a testament to the importance of monogamy and fidelity). The women in *Rock Springs* frequently offer the men a brief companionship, nothing more, nothing less; certainly the men in these stories are rarely alone. The impermanence that this inevitably brings with it is given a physical reflection in the journeys that the characters are often taking (Sims and Marge in 'Empire', Earl and Edna in 'Rock Springs') or are about to take (the narrator of 'Going to the Dogs').

Those male characters who do not obey Russ's moral code (and there is a strong, if unconventional, morality in *Rock Springs*, just as there was in *The Sportswriter*), like narrator

Earl in the title story (who has 'invited trouble' by passing bad cheques) can find themselves in a parking lot late at night trying to decide which car to steal, and separated from the life they feel belongs to them:

> And in the back there were kids' toys and some pillows and a cat box with a cat sitting in it staring up at me like I was the face of the moon. It all looked familiar to me, the very same things I would have in my car if I had a car. Nothing seemed surprising, nothing different.[55]

Yet back in the motel room Earl has a little daughter and a girl-friend who is about to leave him. 'What would you think a man was doing,' Earl asks rhetorically,

> if you saw him in the middle of the night looking in the windows of cars in the parking lot of the Ramada Inn? Would you think he was trying to get his head cleared? Would you think he was trying to get ready for a day when trouble would come down on him? Would you think he had a daughter? Would you think he was anybody like you?[56]

You wouldn't, but you should, seems to be the unspoken answer to the last question; like 'Optimists', 'Rock Springs' conveys powerfully how little it takes to twist not just one life, but several, away from a safe course.

Sometimes the bad luck that befalls the characters takes a bizarre form: in 'Going to the Dogs', a short, strange and very funny story that serves to throw some light into the collection, two fat huntresses dragging a huge deer call on the narrator as he is about to skip to Florida to 'change my luck'.[57] (His wife has run off with a jockey, and he has no money to pay the rent on the house he is using.) The huntresses have come to give the absent landlord a deer steak, but they settle instead for an odd and instant relationship with the tenant, who beds the jollier of the two within minutes of their arrival. Later, when they have gone, the narrator discovers that they have robbed him.

In *The Sportswriter* Frank Bascombe reflects ruefully on the stories he wrote before he abandoned his literary career: 'My characters generally embodied the attitude that life is always going to be a damn nasty and probably baffling business, but somebody has to go on slogging through it.'[58] 'Going to the

Dogs' is full of the kind of touches that prevent Ford's stories from fulfilling Bascombe's description: the strangeness of the central character's predicament, the unpredictable nature of his relationships, the resourceful way the people use the vocabulary at their disposal ('You've got arms like a wheelchair athlete',[59] the jolly fat huntress tells the narrator admiringly). The characters in *Rock Springs* may feel that they must slog through life, but our task is altogether less onerous than the one the younger Bascombe set for his readers.

Wildlife is, as I have said, very much in the 'teenage' series begun in *Rock Springs*. Once again the setting is Great Falls, Montana; again, an adult narrator is looking back on a crucial incident in his life; and again, this incident revolves around trouble between his parents.

The bulk of the narrative takes place over three days. Jerry, the narrator's father, is sacked from his job as a golf coach and goes off to fight the huge forest fires raging just outside the town, leaving his wife Jeanette and son Joe behind. Jeanette immediately becomes involved in an affair with a man called Warren Miller, older than her, and considerably less attractive than her husband, but much wealthier. Jerry returns from the fire, learns of the affair and takes Joe round to Warren Miller's house, which he douses with petrol and sets alight, although no one is hurt.

In many ways Ford is simply expanding on old themes here. Luck makes its customary appearance on the first page: Joe's father took them to Montana during an oil boom, 'and he wanted a piece of that good luck before all of it collapsed and was gone in the wind.'[60] Similarly there is a powerful but familiar sense of the arbitrary in *Wildlife*: we are led to understand that what happens or does not happen to a character is something beyond their control, and there is little or no relationship between fate and personality (a relationship that traditionally underpins much fiction). 'Events can maroon you',[61] says Joe's mother at one point, a perception that many of Ford's characters share.

The multiplicity of options available is confusing, particularly to Joe; when he becomes aware of the nature of his mother's relationship to Miller, he contemplates what options are open to him:

> Now seemed to be a time—the first one in my life—when I needed to know exactly what to do, and out of all the choices I had I wanted to choose the right thing, and start in that direction.[62]

Simply being aware of the dilemma is not enough, however:

> Though there must be times, I thought, when there was no right thing to know, just as there were times when there was no right thing to do. 'Limbo' was the word my mother had used, and that is where I was now, in limbo, between the cares of other people with only my own cares to show me what to do.[63]

'Limbo' is important to the book as a whole. Jeanette describes it as 'The place where nobody wants to be. It's the middle where you can't feel the sides and nothing happens.'[64] It is a bad place to be, yet a place difficult to circumvent. At one point, when Jeanette and Miller are in the man's car making love and Joe is aware of what is happening, he shines a torch onto a magpie through his mother's bedroom window:

> It did not know I was there. It could not feel the light that was on it, couldn't see anything different occurring. It just sat as though it were waiting for something to start to happen that would give it a reason to move or to fly or even look in one direction or the other.[65]

It is a memorable and resonant image which encapsulates the mood of the book; eventually, like the family in 'Optimists', Joe, Jeanette and Jerry have found a reason to move on.

Although *Wildlife* is very much in the mould of the teenage stories in *Rock Springs*, there are a number of noticeable variations and progressions. Jerry's absence at the fire for much of the duration of the book gives Ford the opportunity to place a woman towards the centre of his narrative for the first time, although Jeanette does recall X in her darknesses and occasional penchant for bitter realism. 'Life, life, life, life, life. Life's long'[66] she observes at one point, an observation that recalls Frank Bascombe's wry remarks about the behaviour of the characters in his short stories. And, like X, she sets off a lack of worldliness and a blank optimism in her husband who, she tells Joe, 'has very beautiful intentions'[67] and who assures his son that 'Nothing bad will happen to you.'[68]

At one point Joe recalls his father's golf tip:

> Clear your mind out. You don't have a care in the world. Then everything you hit goes in the hole. It's when you have a lot on your mind, Joe, that you leave everything short.[69]

Golf would thus appear to be the perfect game for Jerry; and working as a golf pro, teaching others to clear their minds out, would appear to be the perfect job.

His decision to leave the family and fight the fire is entirely consistent; indeed, it is a gesture characteristic of a certain strain of Ford male, prompted as it is by a restlessness ('a hum in my head',[70] as Jerry puts it) and a recklessness. (When Warren Miller learns that there are women fighting the fire, he declares that 'Women are better at it than men . . . they know what you're supposed to run from.'[71])

The fire also provides Ford with a potent and terrifying symbol (a device that he has hitherto had little time for; like Frank Bascombe, Ford is more literal than literary). Joe dreams that 'our house had caught fire, a spark travelling miles on a wind and catching our roof, consuming everything'[72]; later, watching the fire with his mother, he comes to understand what the word 'dangerous' means to him. 'It was a thing that did not seem able to hurt you, but quickly and deceivingly would.'[73] Jeanette explains to Joe that 'the whole fire was just a lot of little separate fires [which] blew up together and destroyed everything.'[74] Eventually the little metaphorical fires—Jerry losing his job, Jeanette's dalliance with Warren Miller, the fire itself—come together to form the final literal fire at Miller's house.

Despite Jerry's attempts to destroy his rival's home, and Jeanette's subsequent temporary departure, *Wildlife* ends on a surprisingly upbeat note: Jerry and Jeanette and Joe do not spin off into different worlds, like the family in 'Optimists'. Jeanette returns, and the family manage to live something like their old life, the life they had before Warren Miller and the fire:

Richard Ford

And though they may have both felt that something had died between them . . . they must've felt—both of them—that there was something of themselves, something important, that could not live at all in any other way but by their being together, much as they had been before.[75]

Joe's perception at the beginning of the book, that 'love was permanent, even though it seemed to recede and leave no trace at all'[76] is, after all, a sound one.

Richard Ford is not a regional writer in the same way that, say, Bobbie Ann Mason is a regional writer, in spite of his strong relationship with the mid-west. He is not a native of Montana; he has written books set in his native South, in New Jersey and in Mexico, and only *Rock Springs* and *Wildlife* take place in and around Great Falls. Indeed, these changes of location have proved to be an enormous strength in Ford's work, as they have effectively allowed him to reinvent himself as a writer. Ford's moves around the U.S. (prompted by his wife's job as a town-planner) have provided him with completely new authorial voices; and those who have been fascinated by these changes will perhaps regret Ford's decision to 'write Great Falls into the ground'. *Wildlife* is in many ways a slight extemporization on what has gone before; it may well be that town-planning and the future of one of America's best contemporary writers are inextricably linked.

NOTES

1. *Independent*, 8 July 1989.
2. *Sunday Times*, 7 June 1987.
3. *Observer*, 7 June 1987.
4. Richard Ford, *A Piece of My Heart* (Flamingo, 1988), p. 2.
5. Ibid., p. 77.
6. Ibid., p. 249.
7. *The Times*, 13 June 1987.
8. Ford, *A Piece of My Heart*, p. 229.
9. Ibid., p. 230.
10. *Observer*, 7 September 1986.
11. Quoted by Ford in *The Times*, 13 June 1987.

12. Quoted by Ford in conversation with the author, June 1990.
13. Unpublished interview with Kasia Body.
14. Richard Ford, *The Sportswriter* (Collins Harvill, 1986), p. 16.
15. Ibid., p. 48.
16. Ibid., p. 13.
17. *Guardian*, 17 July 1989.
18. Ford, *The Sportswriter*, p. 54.
19. Ibid., p. 54.
20. Ibid., p. 109.
21. Ibid., p. 134.
22. Ibid., p. 162.
23. Ibid., p. 202.
24. Ibid., p. 235.
25. Ibid., p. 69.
26. Ibid., p. 69.
27. Ibid., p. 210.
28. Ibid., p. 10.
29. Ibid., p. 30.
30. Ibid., p. 10.
31. Ibid., p. 255.
32. Ibid., p. 134.
33. Ibid., p. 135.
34. Ibid., p. 289.
35. Ibid., pp. 288–89.
36. Ibid., p. 146.
37. Ibid., p. 11.
38. Ibid., p. 11.
39. Ibid., p. 165.
40. Ibid., p. 340.
41. Ibid., p. 371.
42. Ibid., p. 373.
43. Ibid., p. 217.
44. Ibid., p. 284.
45. Ibid., p. 218.
46. *New York Times Review of Books*, 7 November 1985.
47. *Independent*, 8 July 1989.
48. *Listener*, 9 August 1990.
49. Richard Ford, *Wildlife* (Collins Harvill, 1991), p. 7.
50. Richard Ford, *Rock Springs* (Collins Harvill, 1988), p. 181.
51. Ibid., p. 198.
52. *Listener*, 9 August 1990.
53. Ford, *Rock Springs*, p. 123.
54. Ibid., p. 78.
55. Ibid., p. 36.
56. Ibid., p. 37.
57. Ibid., p. 109.
58. Ford, *The Sportswriter*, p. 53.
59. Ford, *Rock Springs*, p. 117.

60. Richard Ford, *Wildlife* (Collins Harvill, 1990), p. 7.
61. Ibid., p. 125.
62. Ibid., p. 120.
63. Ibid., p. 121.
64. Ibid., p. 39.
65. Ibid., pp. 105-6.
66. Ibid., p. 73.
67. Ibid., p. 37.
68. Ibid., p. 15.
69. Ibid., p. 105.
70. Ibid., p. 34.
71. Ibid., p. 72.
72. Ibid., p. 11.
73. Ibid., p. 52.
74. Ibid., p. 98.
75. Ibid., p. 162.
76. Ibid., p. 30.

6

Jayne Anne Phillips;
Joy Williams

In many ways Jayne Anne Phillips and Joy Williams provide a missing link between two stages of American fiction. Elsewhere I have quoted Bobbie Ann Mason referring to the way that American writers of the '60s and early '70s—John Barth is an obvious example—turned their backs on the world and produced a body of 'experimental, phantasmagorical'[1] work; Mason believes that the current trend towards realism is a reaction away from that.

Phillips and Williams straddle the two genres quite comfortably, only partly because they both began to publish in the mid-'70s rather than later on in the decade or at the beginning of the next. Both share sufficient common ground with Carver, Wolff *et al.* to have been included in *Granta*'s anthologies, and yet there is a discernibly different set of influences at work here: their companions in the *Granta* collections can be loosely categorized as descendants of the Hemingway school, but these two borrow freely from a variety of traditions to form a sub-group that could be termed 'Dirty Surrealism'.

In *Black Tickets,* Jayne Anne Phillips' first collection of stories, these traditions have a tendency to appear side by side, as yet undigested, although their range and apparent disparity is such that the authorial voice thus created is refreshingly unique in contemporary American writing. *Black Tickets* consists of twenty-seven stories, although over half of them are less than a page long. This in itself constitutes an American tradition: in 1986 Penguin published a book entitled *Sudden Fiction*, an anthology of 'American short-short stories' from such writers as Joyce Carol Oates, Updike, Barry Hannah, Max Apple and Gordon Lish, as well as Carver and Wolff. In Robert Shapard's introduction, he describes these 'short-shorts' as 'highly compressed, highly-charged, insidious, protean, sudden'; they 'can do in a page what a novel does in two hundred.'[2]

This claim is, of course, pure hyperbole, and in any case it does not appear to me to be Phillips' intention in *Black Tickets*. The 'short-shorts' are carefully organized so that they throw light on the longer pieces of work that invariably follow them (this sort of cross-currenting is a feature of Phillips' work); themes and images and language 'leak' from one to another.

Thus the collection begins with 'Wedding Picture' and 'Home'. The first is a three-paragraph description of a photograph of the narrator's mother and father. It serves not only as an introduction to the writer's opaque prose, which in its richness and rhythm borrows much from contemporary poetry ('My father's heart pounds, a bell in a wrestler's chest. He is almost forty and the lilies are trumpeting.'[3]), but to alert us to the preoccupations of one strand of the writer's work.

'Home', the longer work, contains deliberate echoes of its predecessor. The narrator examines photographs of her mother; just as in the first story, a link is made between sickness and marriage. In 'Home' the narrator has returned to live with her mother temporarily ('I ran out of money and I wasn't in love, so I have come home. . .'[4]). There is another chapter in this book devoted to the classic *New Yorker*-style women's short story detailing emotional and domestic dislocation, but 'Home' is emphatically not of this genre; Phillips achieves a foreboding, almost apocalyptic tone through a procession of references to disease (the narrator's mother is obsessed with the notion that various celebrities have cancer), war (the narrator's old lover, who visits her at her mother's house, bears horrendous scars incurred in Vietnam), and indeed the Apocalypse itself—the narrator watches *On the Beach*, the old Gregory Peck film about the last few humans to survive a nuclear attack, with the sound turned down.

This unremittingly bleak scenario serves as a frame for the first of the writer's many explorations into sexuality—if 'Home' is 'about' anything in the conventional sense, it is about sex—but it is a disturbed and disturbing version of the theme. The tone is set by the narrator's dream of her father:

> He presses himself against my thigh, pretending solicitude. But I know what he is doing; I turn my head in repulsion and stiffen. He smells of a sour musk and his forearms are black with hair. I think to myself, it's been years since he's had an erection. . . .[5]

The sex between the narrator and her ex-lover Daniel is initially thwarted by the oppressive surroundings ('I can't breathe in here', says Daniel[6]); the noise of their eventual coupling creates the tension between mother and daughter left unresolved at the end of the story:

> I heard you, I heard it, she says. Here, in my own house. Please, how much can you expect me to take? I don't know what to do about anything.
> She looks into the water, keeps looking. And we stand here just like this.[7]

There are generational conflicts in 'Home'—the mother is appalled by her daughter's promiscuity—but the narrator also refers to their 'telepathy': 'Before her hysterectomy, our periods often came on the same day.'[8] It is this mutual identification that gives a different dimension to the story and its components (the incestual dream, for example, and the mother's alternating fascination for and horror of the sex act).

In his book *Looka Yonder!*, Duncan Webster draws attention to the 'ambiguity at the core of the myth of the American road: travelling as freedom or travelling as a necessary escape, something imposed not chosen'.[9] In 'Home' the narrator recalls how her mother 'sent me to college, she paid for my safe escape'; it is an escape imposed by the spectre of the father, 'his ghost with its cigarette burning in the dark like a sore.' Part of the point of the story, and the source of its darkness, is that the escape has failed: 'Home' is the flip side of the road myth, and in its diseased narrative recalls Gramsci's observation that 'when the old dies and the new cannot be born, a variety of morbid symptoms appear.'

A story placed towards the end of the collection, 'Souvenir', is preceded by another 'short-short', the one-paragraph 'Strangers in the Night', which links sex and death in a way reminiscent of 'Home'. The longer story is an example of Phillips at her least poetic (and in many ways her least interesting, at least stylistically). However, the story does show a similar movement towards a synthesis of parent and child. 'You're sick, aren't you',[10] asks a dying mother of her adult daughter; once again, the two women somehow confuse each other, and there are echoes that bounce between the two women similar to the ones that bounce between the two stories.

'Souvenir' and 'Home' show signs of the mainstream influences of contemporary American short fiction, even if their themes belong uniquely to Phillips. Elsewhere, however, particularly in 'Lechery', 'El Paso' and the title story, the writer's prose shows that its roots also lie in the 'Beat' writing of Kerouac and Kesey, and occasionally recalls the dizzying, drug-addled textures of Burroughs:

> But days were best. Days were OK. I stood across the street watching you and waiting to make the drop. At first it was sideline stuff, Nembies and speed balls, a little white stuff for the joy bangers who came down-town to cop.[11]

The junkie demotic is certainly a throw-back to *Naked Lunch*-era Burroughs, but Phillips is a more convincing writer; she is certainly more ambitious.

'Black Tickets' is a hymn from an imprisoned drug-runner to his one-time girl-friend, who sold tickets in the crumbling cinema used by the pushers for clandestine sales. It is a complex, difficult and occasionally obscure story, but Phillips' real achievement here is again an essentially synthetic one, in the true sense of the word; she grafts a new, dark vision of a populist America onto the old one of film and popular music:

> I bought a ticket from you, threw the money in that cupped slot and saw your fingernails, blackish violet, catch the silver faces of the quarters. I went inside. Obelisk. The bathrooms were big, horsehair sofa and fan-man carpets worn through, then the white tile floors broken and chipped till the border mosaics were cracked to an ivory powder. We used to cut speed with that powder; all those silky Main Line debs reeling in their mommy's sports cars, digesting the crumbling universe of Obelisk.[12]

Thus the crumbling old America is physically ingested by the new; the old palliatives have been ground down to dust, and are sold as make-weights by their previous consumers.

'El Paso', the strongest story in the first collection, is set in 1965, but this sense of a community in decay is equally strong. The tale of a brief, intense love affair between 'Dude' and Rita, the shifting relationships between characters, and between characters and place, is underlined by the frequent change in narrator. Dude meets Rita on a farm, while in the process of buying her father's truck (Rita's colloquial and obscure account of life on the farm, complete with its portrait of her witchily deformed baby brother, is a piece of Southern Gothic reminiscent of Faulkner), and takes her into the town with him. She dances in a bar for a while, with occasional prostitution work on the side; Dude ends up peddling hash. The story has an archetypal quality to it: The Blond, one of Rita's colleagues, has travelled from Maine to Mexico and back up to Texas, and her anonymity and restlessness seem intended to confer an almost mythical status upon her.

In a sense 'El Paso' is a summation of the twin themes of movement and stasis in *Black Tickets*—in effect, 'Home' and the road. Staying put has strong associations with decay:

> It was plain he wanted to go off with her but in the summer in El Paso it's hard to move anywhere except down the street to the bars. I remember there was always dog puke on the sidewalks in El Paso.[13]

The relationship between Rita and Dude ends in violence, and inevitably Dude gets away as quickly as he can. Movement, however, provides only the temporary illusion of freedom:

> I saw him a couple of years later in Toledo, said he was into racing junk cars, said it was some kick. Said you're tearing around and around under the lights in these things that are all going to fly apart and pile up. Said he heard she was living down in Austin with some dyke. Said cracking up those cars was great, said he was making some money and cracking them up was some kick, it was really something.[14]

Dude's edgy, repetitive, enervated speech rhythms, and the metaphor of the junk cars, suggest that this kind of frantic escape is no more effective a response to modern America than sitting in dingy Texas bars in the heat.

The opposition between home and the road is confronted more explicitly in the title story from Phillips' second collection, *Fast Lanes*, in which the two central characters, Thurman and the (woman) narrator, temporarily abandon their wandering life-style in order to return to their home-towns and parents. 'When I met Thurman,' says the narrator, 'he was floating and I was floating home'[15]; as Duncan Webster has pointed out, 'We are one stage on from drifting, floating shows even fewer ties to solidity.'[16]

Much of the language used in connection with home is familiar to us from previous Phillips stories; for the narrator, going back is hard because 'sometimes it's hard to breathe, like living under blankets. . . . Hot, but cold too. Shaking.'[17] (Daniel in 'Home' had the same problems.) When the couple reach Thurman's parents' home, the narrator notices that the rooms 'smelled of faded potpourri and trapped air, despite the air-conditioner'.[18] And the house itself shows signs of the stasis that we have come to expect: preparations have been made for repainting, but Thurman explains that this happened some years ago, and nothing has happened.

As in *Black Tickets*, Phillips fuses the tokens of American popular culture onto something altogether more ambiguous. Thurman's memories of watching Doris Day movies at the local cinema, for example, contextualize the experience:

> His two older brothers kissed girls in the balcony while he sat in the back row downstairs with the Mexicans. Blue-eyed Doris flickered in a bad print to the tune of bubbly music and wetback jeers. Thurman said he liked Doris in those days because she was so out-of-it she made no sense to anyone,

and she kept raising her eyebrows, perky, not quite smart, as
wads of paper and popcorn boxes bounced off the screen.[19]

This version of an American icon (Doris Day is the paradigmatic 'hometown girl' in the mythical sense of the expression) is widened to include its consumption in a way that prevents it from operating symbolically in the lives of Phillips' characters.

Thurman's experience of playing for his school football team is similarly iconoclastic. His last game resulted in a massive head injury:

> Football nearly killed me. I couldn't read print for two weeks. . . . But even without the concussion, I was sick of it. I went to Colorado and ski-bummed and ran dope up from Mexico. . . .[20]

Later, Thurman recalls that when his football-playing brother was killed in Vietnam, his father firmly believed that the boy must have been taking drugs: 'They're all on drugs over there. He wouldn't have died otherwise, he was an athlete.'

'Fast Lanes', however, is as much about the narrator's ability to survive her floating life-style as it is about the underbelly of the home-town myth. She is younger than Thurman, who, at 30, has lived as an adult through the crucial second half of the '60s and its aftermath (the story is set in 1975), and thus feels qualified to pass on advice, in a conversation that provides the story and the collection with its title:

> 'Don't drive in the fast lane unless you're passing.' Thurman, his voice gravelly with wakefulness.
> 'Why not? I pass everything anyway, so I might as well stay in the fast lane. I like fast lanes.'
> 'Oh, you do. Well someone even faster is going to come roaring up and eat your ass. How will you like that.'[21]

This metaphor is given weight by the narrator's unspecified experience in a motel room with three strangers who pick her up in a bar: 'What happened was scary and stupid, and whirling and sick and drunkenly predictable.'[22] Again, the kind of escape offered to Phillips' characters is an imposed one, and offers no freedom (especially, perhaps, for women) other than that of constant and wearying movement.

The counterpart to 'Fast Lanes' is 'Blue Moon', which

is Phillips' most explicit story about community in the same way that the title story is her most explicit story about movement. 'Blue Moon' contains an echo of 'Wedding Picture', the first 'short-short' in *Black Tickets*: Jean, the mother of the central characters, had a high school boy-friend who died of a heart attack after a football game. This is an apparent illumination of an oblique reference in the earlier story: 'Five years since the high school lover crumpled on the bathroom floor, his sweet heart raw.'[23]

'Blue Moon' is a 'home' story, then, but it is nevertheless fixated with the idea of escape. Jean and her family—husband Mitch and teenage children Billy and Danner—live in Bellington, an archetypal American one-horse town, where the local high school provides a focus to the community. For the young people (including Billy's girl-friend Kato) the idea of elsewhere is strong, but the routes away are typically unattractive; Billy is about to go to military school, and thence to Vietnam, and by the end of the story, Kato too is out of Bellington, in Dayton, Ohio—but only because she has slashed herself with a blunt knife and has been sent to a relative to recover. The summer before the events in the narrative, Danner had slept with a boy for the first time, ostensibly because '. . . it made me feel as though I weren't in Bellington anymore.'[24] 'It feels like the world has ended', Kato's father Shinner tells her at the end of the story, 'But you kids are not like us. You won't always live here. Already, you're practically gone.'[25]

In some ways, Phillips' ideas on the end of the American community are reminiscent of Bobbie Ann Mason's work; but whereas Mason's stories have a political dimension to them, and are therefore concerned with the literal reality of movement, there is a metaphysical dimension to Phillips' writing. The central metaphor in 'Blue Moon' is of a trampoline—Billy represents the school at gymnastics—and Phillips finds a number of resonant uses for it. Obviously one meaning here involves movement (one of Billy's books has a chapter headed 'Values: More Than Any Other Activity, Trampolining Develops a Sense of Relocation'[26]), yet the escape it offers is illusory, resulting as it does in a return to earth. And the activity necessitates solipsism (Billy is forbidden by his mother to play team games) and alienation ('Billy wanted to do things no one in Bellington had ever seen anyone do'[27]). There is a sense in which Phillips takes a theme central to American fiction and makes it pertain to the psyche of the individual rather than, as is more usually the case, of the country.

It is difficult to imagine why Joy Williams was chosen to represent the new realist school of fiction in *Granta 19: More Dirt*. Her contribution to that collection, 'Escapes' (the title story of her second book of short fiction) is much more reminiscent of Donald Barthelme, the influential '70s' surrealist, than it is of Hemingway: there is the same quasi-surreal narrative style, and a similar penchant for strange, disconnected dialogue. Neither taste exhibits much respect for the conventions of the dominant realist mode of current American fiction.

In 'The Wedding' (from Williams' first collection, *Taking Care*) it is clear that the author has been influenced by the '70s' fabulism of authors such as John Barth ('Elizabeth always wanted to read fables to her little girl. . .', the story begins[28]). 'The Wedding' is studded with references to a number of fairy tales—'Little Red Riding Hood', 'The Frog King'—and other forms of escapist fantasy: the film *Captain Blood*, with Errol Flynn, for example. It soon becomes apparent that 'The Wedding' is essentially metafictional in intent—it is a story about stories—and is self-referential in a way that those writers discussed elsewhere in this book have rejected. When Elizabeth's attempts to recount a tale are met with impatient interruptions from her daughter and Sam, her lover, she responds with what amounts to a self-conscious articulation of the author's (ironically old-fashioned, given the understatement characteristic of much American short fiction) post-modern concerns:

> Elizabeth says, 'There were two men wrecked on a desert island and one of them pretended he was home while the other admitted. . . .'
> 'Oh Mummy,' the child says.
> 'I know that one,' Sam says from the tub. 'They both died.'

'This is not a primitive story,' Elizabeth says. 'Colorless, anticlimactic endings are typical only of primitive stories.'[29] And as an ironic consequence of Elizabeth's analysis, 'The Wedding' ends with a glorious climactic vision, a parodic version of the mother's romantic preoccupations. Sam and Elizabeth marry: 'Together, in their animistic embrace, they float out the window and circle the house, gazing down at all those who have not found true love, below.'[30]

There are several elements here typical of the author's work: the erudition of her vocabulary, for example (it is difficult to imagine Carver or Ford choosing to use the word 'animistic'), the surprising and fantastical conclusion; these elements in themselves are enough to suggest that Williams' fiction springs from sources unexplored by many of those erroneously regarded as her stablemates.

The range of moods on display in *Taking Care* lays to rest any suspicion that Williams is merely a fictional theoretician (and in any case her wry, dry commentary, artfully concealed, on the aspirations of women does provide 'The Wedding' with an extra dimension). The opening story, 'The Lover', is as dark and unnerving as some of Jayne Anne Phillips' work, with its portrayal of a woman whose only connection with the outside world is via her radio, which can only receive one station. Again, the story possesses a surreal, anti-naturalistic component: the woman, waiting for a lover who may or may not reappear, listens night after night to a programme featuring the Answer Man, who replies to the questions that listeners ring in with. Sometimes these questions are banal ('Could you tell me why the filling in my lemon meringue pie is runny?'[31]); sometimes they are unheard, but elicit strange and ominous responses: 'The wine of this world has caused only satiety. Our homes suffer from female sadness, embarrassment and confusion. Absense, sterility, mourning, privation and separation abound throughout the land.'[32]

Cynics might argue that this last sentence is an adequate summation of the entire output of many contemporary American women writers. True, there is an element of bleak portentousness in stories like 'The Lover', but it is important not to overlook Williams' wry humour or her irony. 'I want to know my hour', says the woman when she 'phones the Answer Man herself. 'Your hour came, dear', he says. 'It went when you were sleeping. It came and saw you dreaming and it went back to where it was.'[33] If Williams' characters are victims, then many of them are victims of a self-induced languid paralysis.

The woman in 'The Lover' has a young daughter, and in this first collection the relationship between parents and children is of paramount importance. Often—as in 'The Lover' and 'The Wedding'—the stories deal with single women apparently unequipped emotionally to cope with their charges (a theme carried over into the title story of the second collection, 'Escapes', where an alcoholic mother takes her child to a magic show and invades the stage). The title story of the first book, however, enters different territory, and the author drops her obliquely censorious tone.

'Taking Care' does feature an emotionally incapable mother, the daughter of Jones, a preacher and the central character in the story:

> Jones's daughter has fallen in with the stars and is using the heavens, as Jones would be the first to admit, more than he ever has. It has, however, brought her only grief and confusion. She has left her husband and brought the baby to Jones. She has also given him her dog. She is going to Mexico where soon, in the mountains, she will have a nervous breakdown.[34]

The plight of the daughter is not germane to the story, even though the collection as a whole is littered with such tales; 'Taking Care' deals with Jones, his dying wife, and his relationship with his grandchild. The story's opening, surprisingly direct, serves as a sombre encapsulation of much of what has preceded it (the title story is placed last in the book):

> Jones, the preacher, has been in love all his life. He is baffled by this, because as far as he can see, it has never helped anyone, even when they have acknowledged it, which is not often. Jones's love is much too apparent and arouses neglect. He is like an animal in a travelling show who, through some aberration, wears a vital organ outside the skin, awkward and unfortunate, something that shouldn't be seen, certainly something that shouldn't be watched working.[35]

Many of Williams' characters are possessed of this 'aberration'. Part of our discomfort when reading 'The Lover' springs from that story's lack of dynamism: the woman waits for her lover and listens to the radio, and in so doing she misses her 'hour'. It is something that 'shouldn't be watched working', but Williams forces us to look. Jones is afflicted with a similar sense of time wasted. 'Have so many years really passed?', he wonders when he sees his dying wife. 'Is this not his wife, his love, fresh from giving birth? Isn't everything about to begin?'[36] At the story's epiphanic ending, he leads his wife back into their home, which he has made spotless. But the quasi-mysticism of the conclusion is slyly inadequate, and hardly compensates for the bleak and bewildering pain of the impending loss. (Williams returns to these characters in her second collection. 'Bromeliads' is a kind of prequel to 'Taking Care', describing how it was that Jones and his wife came to be looking after the baby. The wife's sickness is at an earlier stage, but the story's preoccupations are similar to those of its predecessor.)

Death is a central theme of a number of the stories in *Escapes*. 'The Skater' and 'The Little Winter' (this link between ice and mortality also features in the first collection, notably in the powerful 'Winter Chemistry'; it should be pointed out that Williams comes from Florida, 'the Sunshine State'). In 'The Skater', a teenage girl, Mollie, and her parents, Tom and Annie, visit a number of potential boarding-schools in a frozen New England. Mollie's sister Martha died in a bizarre and shocking fashion a year previously (she choked on a piece of bread while listening to the radio; 'two disc jockeys called the Breakfast Flakes chattered away between songs'[37]).

'The Skater' is about the difficulty, or even the impossibility, of coping with loss. Shortly after the death, Annie puts on one of Martha's favourite caps: 'She thought it would help her feel closer to Martha but it didn't. The sweatband smelled slightly of shampoo, but it was just a cap.'[38] And later, when Annie remarks on a visit that 'Martha would like this school, wouldn't she?', Tom replies simply: 'We don't know, Annie. Please don't, Annie.'[39] It is as if the cold that permeates the story deadens the resonances of the loss.

Ironically, however, it is the cold that provides the surviving members of the family with a way of connecting with

Martha. When Mollie is taken to see a skating rink at one of the schools, she notices that it is overlooked by a large, badly painted portrait of a skater, a boy who, she learns, died some years previously. Mollie feels compelled to tell the guide, untruthfully, that Martha knew him.

> She thinks of Martha and Jimmy Watkins being together, telling each other secrets. They will like each other. They are seventeen and fourteen, living in the single moment that they have been gone.[40]

Thus Mollie finds a way to enshrine her sister, and the portrait becomes an oblique memorial.

Tom and Annie, in another delicately redemptive conclusion, find a similar route, although it is Williams' symbolism, rather than their own awareness, that allows this release. Tom walks out onto the ice at a lakeside hotel and attempts to slide; from a window Mollie watches 'her mother moving towards him, not skating, but slipping forward, making her way. She sees their heavy awkward shapes embrace.'[41] Williams' metaphors are understated and complex, but the hope offered to the depleted family by Mollie's vision is unmistakeable.

The central character in 'The Little Winter', Gloria, is terminally ill with a brain tumour, although this information is withheld until the middle of the story. 'The Little Winter' is perhaps the supreme example of Williams' unique voice, because although it is of necessity occasionally melancholic, the writer perversely chooses to utilize her wry, bizarre humour. The title refers to the 'false' season which occurs in Gloria's home state before the onset of the real thing:

> When she was small they had lived in a place where the little winter came first. That's what everyone called it. There was 'the little winter', then there were pleasant days, sometimes even weeks. Then the big winter came. She felt dreamy and cold, a little disconnected from everything.[42]

This metaphor recurs in more explicit form later in the story ('Back in the desert, just before she had made this trip, she had had her little winter'[43]); thus the events described in the story are 'the pleasant days', and the last sentence of the above quotation refers, with a wonderful dry irony, to Gloria's imminent death.

In many ways the story is *about* understatement and euphemism. To Gloria death is by implication 'the big winter'; to Gwendal, the 10-year-old daughter of Gloria's friend Jean, it is 'The Great Adventure'[44] or 'The Big Surprise'.[45] The last paragraph of the story describes Gloria's jumbled frustration with her own inarticulacy: 'She wanted to say something but even that wasn't it. She didn't want to say anything. She wanted to realize something she couldn't say.'[46] Throughout the story the language of the characters is inadequate for the experience—a recurring theme in current American literature, although rarely approached with as much sophistication or wit as Williams does here.

Perhaps the strangest story in *Escapes*, 'Rot', also touches on death and mortality, but Williams' approach is even more whimsical than in 'The Little Winter'. Synopsized, the story makes Williams sound like the worst kind of Beckett-obsessive: Lucy's husband Dwight buys a crumbling Ford Thunderbird (when he found the car, its owner was dead at the wheel, and he bought it from the next of kin); and because he is unable to drive it, he removes a wall of their house and places it in their living room. But despite the apparent reference to European symbolism, 'Rot' is a fresh version of mainstream themes in American fiction.

Dwight is considerably older than Lucy, whom he first met when she was a baby and he was 25, and this difference is crucial in their relationship. When Dwight first brings the Thunderbird home, he points out that his wife and the car are the same age; thus it immediately takes on metaphorical significance, and the words of Boris, the mechanic invited to inspect it, take on an extra dimension:

> My suggestion is to drive this car, . . . enjoy it, but for the spring and summer only, then dump it, part it out. Otherwise, you'll be putting in new welds, but always the collapse will be just ahead of you. Years will pass and then will come the day when there is nothing to weld the weld to, there is no frame, nothing. Once rot, then nothing.[47]

'Rot' thus becomes a masterpiece of fertile and resourceful comic imagery, and the mechanic's speech seems to refer to Dwight's careful use of women as a kind of regeneration. A procession of his ex-girl-friends walk through the story: Caroline, who is with Dwight when he buys the car, and tells Lucy (in a foreshadowing of the mechanic's elaborately emblematic warning) that she acted as its horn ('I'd yell out the window. . .'[48]); Daisy, ten years older than Lucy (and thus still considerably younger than Dwight), who has lost a leg; Rosette, whose marriage to Bob is in a state of disrepair. It would appear that Dwight has been putting in new welds in an attempt to stave off the threatened imminent collapse.

Dwight's decision to ignore the advice of Boris and bring the car indoors is in effect a bizarre expression of his love for Lucy, and demonstrates his intended fidelity.

> She's a honey but she's tired. Elements are hard on a car. . . . We'll keep her shined up and sit inside her and talk. It's very peaceful inside that little car, you know.[49]

When Lucy does sit inside the care for the first time, however, her interpretation of the action is more cynical: 'I had the tiniest feeling in there that the point being made was that something has robbed this world of its promise.'[50]

At the end of the story Lucy has begun to understand the car's significance:

> It wasn't just a question of moving this used-up thing out again, she knew that. Time was moving sideways the way it had always seemed to her to move but was climbing upward, then falling back, then lurching in a circle like some poisoned, damaged thing.[51]

'Rot' is a story which exhibits Williams' particular skills to their best effect. It is complex and funny, yet there is an underlying sadness in Dwight's berserk attempts to ward off decay. And the use of car symbolism is in itself worthy of discussion: as Duncan Webster has pointed out, the road has long been an ambivalent theme in American fiction, and here, with her symbol of a rusting, stationary vehicle, Williams provides an ironic counterpoint to its more commonplace resonances. (The car also provides an ironic commentary on the title she has chosen for the collection, as it simultaneously represents both escape and its impossibility.) And we should remain aware that car imagery and its attendant virility has been a predominantly male preserve (the songs of American singer Bruce Springsteen have become almost notorious in this respect); the ultimate irony of 'Rot' is that a woman writer should use a Thunderbird to illustrate a male's fear of death.

Elsewhere I have discussed the particular kind of short story that has come to represent contemporary American women's fiction, but Jayne Anne Phillips and Joy Williams represent an important challenge to this hegemony. Phillips has a darkness to her work that is currently unique, and the range of her voices has a breadth that cannot be found in a literary landscape dominated by the homogenous teaching of the creative writing schools. Williams has a humour and absurdism that makes her writing immediately identifiable, and, as we have seen, her elaborate symbolism is a welcome variance on the literalist approaches of other recent story-writers. It is perhaps not surprising that neither author has as yet managed to produce a wholly successful novel, although Williams' *Breaking and Entering* is an interesting expansion on some of the themes in her short fiction; the intensity of their work, Phillips' bleak passion and Williams' extraordinarily finely-wrought detail, inevitably translate uneasily to the longer form. But there is a brief history of contemporary American writing to be found in collections like *Fast Lanes* and *Escapes*, and it is this plurality of influence that students of their work will find particularly rewarding.

NOTES

1. See p. 90.
2. Robert Shaphard and James Thomas (eds.), *Sudden Fiction* (Penguin, 1986), p. xvi.
3. Jayne Anne Phillips, *Black Tickets* (Penguin, 1988), p. 4.
4. Ibid., p. 8.
5. Ibid., p. 12.
6. Ibid., p. 21.
7. Ibid., p. 25.

8. Ibid., p. 15.
9. Duncan Webster, *Looka Yonder! The Imaginary America of Populist Culture* (Comedia/Routledge, 1988), p. 118.
10. Phillips, p. 196.
11. Ibid., p. 53.
12. Ibid., p. 53.
13. Ibid., p. 83.
14. Ibid., pp. 84–5.
15. Jayne Anne Phillips, *Fast Lanes* (Faber, 1988), p. 41.
16. Webster, p. 118.
17. Phillips, p. 44.
18. Ibid., p. 54.
19. Ibid., p. 40.
20. Ibid., p. 56.
21. Ibid., p. 60.
22. Ibid., p. 60.
23. Jayne Anne Phillips, *Black Tickets* (Penguin 1988), p. 4.
24. Phillips, *Fast Lanes*, p. 98.
25. Ibid., p. 121.
26. Ibid., p. 110.
27. Ibid., p. 91.
28. Joy Williams, *Taking Care* (New York: Random House, 1982), p. 39.
29. Ibid., p. 46.
30. Ibid., p. 48.
31. Ibid., p. 4.
32. Ibid., p. 6.
33. Ibid., p. 10.
34. Ibid., p. 234.
35. Ibid., p. 233.
36. Ibid., p. 243.
37. Joy Williams, *Escapes* (Collins Harvill, 1990), p. 34.
38. Ibid., p. 38.
39. Ibid., p. 39.
40. Ibid., p. 43.
41. Ibid., p. 45.
42. Ibid., pp. 77–8.
43. Ibid., p. 93.
44. Ibid., p. 94.
45. Ibid., p. 91.
46. Ibid., p. 95.
47. Ibid., p. 23.
48. Ibid., p. 15.
49. Ibid., p. 28.
50. Ibid., p. 29.
51. Ibid., p. 32.

7
Tobias Wolff

Tobias Wolff is in many ways the most straightforward of American contemporary short-story writers. There is no regional bias in his stories, and nor does one particular section of society populate them; in his first collection, *Hunters in the Snow*, the cast of central characters includes a couple of college professors, a teenage delinquent, a salesman and a cartoonist. Unlike Ford and Carver, he is concerned with language only in the traditional sense: that is to say, he uses words in a resolutely pre-modern way, as a window through which to see the world, and there are none of the awkward, alienating phrases or snatches of dialogue that his two more celebrated colleagues delight in. His range and his traditionalism have meant that he has been somewhat unfairly overlooked, particularly in the U.K., but in fact he does possess a distinctive and interesting voice whose plainness is its strength, rather than an indication that it has nothing to add to the fictional din being produced across the Atlantic.

His fictional output so far has been relatively meagre (which may in part explain his relative anonymity here): two slim volumes of short stories, *Hunters in the Snow* and *Back in the World*; a longer piece, 'The Barracks Thief' (first published in *Granta 8: Dirty Realism*); and a memoir, *This Boy's Life*.

What is immediately apparent from the first collection is that there is a strong moral sense at work in Wolff's fiction; and although others in his peer group (particularly Richard Ford) have been termed moralists, Wolff's morality is of a more conventional kind. It is thus easier to draw a line from Wolff through Cheever and O'Hara right back to O. Henry and Twain than it is to link Ford, Carver *et al.* in with such an American tradition.

One of the first stories in this first collection, 'An Episode in the Life of Professor Brooke', exemplifies this strain in Wolff's work. The story begins with a brief outline of Professor Brooke's antipathy towards Riley, one of his colleagues in the English department; this dislike stems from the fact that Riley (who attends the same church as Brooke) is an apparently notorious seducer of the female students. Brooke's wife is charitable in her interpretation of an incident in which a girl was spotted leaving Riley's office in tears, but Brooke only pretends to agree with her. Suddenly, however, Brooke finds himself embarking upon a one-night stand, for more or less impeccable reasons: the woman he beds at a conference has trusted him enough to remove a wig that she wears following chemotherapy, and Brooke tells her how attractive he finds her. For months after the incident he receives anonymous love letters, to which he offers no response; in the meantime he has deceived his wife, who is aware (as is the adulterer Riley) that something of this nature has taken place on Brooke's trip.

If most modern American short-story writers end their works with, as one reviewer puts it, 'infinitesimal shifts in consciousness', Wolff is atypical: in his stories things happen, people change, and 'An Episode in the Life of Professor Brooke' ends with characters both older and wiser, and even with that most unfashionable of conclusions, a moral—although Wolff attempts to disguise it with a modish little meta-fictional flourish:

> Without really being aware of it, Brooke saw the events of his life as forming chapters, and when he felt a chapter drawing to a close he liked to tie it up with an appropriate sentiment. Never again, he decided, would he sit in the back of the church and watch Riley. From now on he would sit in the front of the church and let Riley, knowing what he knew, watch him. He would kneel before Riley as we must all, he thought, kneel before one another.[1]

This final line gets to the heart of much of Wolff's fiction. Its overt spirituality may stem from the fact that the author has in recent years rediscovered Catholicism: 'I found myself getting interested in the Church again and eventually was confirmed. Now it's very much a part of my life', he told Paul Ryan in 1988.[2] Although the idea of judgement as contained in 'An Episode in the Life of Professor Brooke' is rarely expressed as directly elsewhere, particularly in the first collection, there is an equivalent story, 'The Rich Brother', in *Back in the World*—as if Wolff requires a central tale in each book to set some kind of moral tone.

'The Rich Brother' (and the title is, perhaps deliberately, parable-like) deals with two brothers, Donald and Pete. Donald is in effect a drop-out (Wolff, uncharacteristically for someone of his generation, seems fiercely negative towards anything that smacks of the counter-culture; I shall discuss further examples of this later). He has been living amongst a religious community on a farm, although most of the story deals with his journey back from it with Pete following his expulsion. Pete is older and materially very comfortable, and Donald seems constantly appalled by his brother's conspicuous consumption.

As in 'An Episode in the Life of Professor Brooke', however, Wolff complexifies the moral issues thrown up by this initially simple scenario: Pete is in every sense his brother's keeper, and Donald's puritanism (like Brooke's) is shown to be irritatingly self-indulgent. He has been expelled from the community from giving away all their groceries to those more deserving; and when Pete gives him $100 to tide him over, he hands it to a charlatan. In effect he is a holy fool, and at the end of the story it becomes clear that Pete, for all his shallowness, has the better adjusted moral sense: the last paragraph of 'The Rich Brother' shows him to be wearily aware that he must go back to collect his brother from the roadside, where he has left him in a fit of frustration, and that he is burdened with a responsibility towards him.

Elsewhere there is a similar concern with right and wrong, but the issues raised are not resolved in the same straightforward manner. 'The Liar' is reminiscent in its merciless clarity of *This Boy's Life*, Wolff's memoir. The liar of the title is a teenage boy whose compulsion to spin wild mistruths about himself and his family prompts his mother to send him to a doctor. Wolff again tries a small twist in an attempt to subvert an accepted moral order: one of the lies the boy tells his mother is to prevent her from discovering that her husband did not die in his bed, as she fondly believes. This is, fortunately, not the essence of 'The Liar', however; the boy's strange redemption comes on a bus that has broken down, when he entertains the passengers by speaking to them in what they believe to be Tibetan (he has told them that he has been working with Tibetan refugees, and that his parents were killed by the Communists):

> They bent towards me. The windows suddenly went blind with rain. The driver had fallen asleep and was snoring gently to the swaying of the bus. Outside the muddy light flickered to pale yellow, and far off there was thunder. The woman next to me leaned back and closed her eyes and then so did all the others as I sang to them in what was surely an ancient and holy tongue.[3]

This kind of quasi-mystical pitch is repeated in the first story of the second collection, 'Coming Attractions', which is a counterpart to 'The Liar' in the same way that 'The Rich Brother' is a counterpart to the Professor Brooke story. 'Coming Attractions' also features a mischievous and unbalanced teenager. The girl has to wait for a lift back from her job in a cinema; she fills the time by 'phoning an old teacher to tell him that he has won a prize, and that she has been involved in a sexual relationship with one of his colleagues. She too is provided with a kind of redemption for her compulsion; the story ends with a vivid description of her attempt to rescue a bicycle from the bottom of a swimming pool for her little brother. It is winter, and the pool is freezing, and the bike is heavy, but she persists until she has brought it to the surface.

Although Wolff is not from the South, it seems to me that in this mode, where his central characters are granted an eccentric but convincing salvation of sorts, he is more reminiscent of Flannery O'Connor than is anyone else discussed in this volume—despite the fact that O'Connor's name is mentioned in nearly every review of every contemporary Southerner. Perhaps a shared faith is more important than geographical accident.

A number of critics have drawn attention to the fact that Wolff's stories can occasionally be quite uncomfortable to read. (Picador's collection of his work uses a quotation which claims they 'recall the eerie menace of Peter Bowles', although perhaps the quote should refer to Paul Bowles, the Morocco-based American author of *The Sheltering Sky*, rather than to the English comedy actor.) Precisely how Wolff achieves this effect is interesting. It would appear to be very much connected with the ambivalence shown towards the central characters in each of the stories, so that we are lured into identifying with someone—often the narrator—whom we end up disliking. Consequently the overwhelming impression at the end of the stories is that Wolff is judging the reader—and himself—as much as he is judging his (anti-) hero.

'An Episode in the Life of Professor Brooke' is one example of this technique at work; 'Smokers', from the first collection, is another. It starts deceptively: when the narrator meets the loud and painful Eugene on a train on the way to their first term in a new school, we presume that Eugene will be the story's focus. We identify with the narrator's embarrassment when his new acquaintance bursts into song in the carriage, and we wince at his Alpine hat with feathers in the brim. Slowly, however, the direction of the narrative changes, and the first-person in the story, with whom we have already struck up some kind of understanding, is revealed as a remorseless, relentless social climber who tramples all over Eugene to get to Talbot, his rich and glamorous friend. The narrator eventually succeeds in getting Eugene expelled from the school, thus leaving the field clear for him to cement the coveted friendship.

Wolff's use of the first person here is powerful and unusual, if not unique (many of Cheever's narrators—Johnny Hake in 'The Housebreaker of Shady Hill', for example—are hardly sympathetic); fiction which attempts to disclose the more unattractive characteristics of human nature is more effective when the reader is forced to acknowledge these characteristics in himself, and the logic of stories like 'Smokers' creates a painful honesty. 'If I can't discover something when I'm writing that scares me a little bit in terms of what it means for me, then the story never comes alive',[4] Wolff once said, and the sour taste that stories like 'Smokers' leave with us is a testament to this kind of self-analysis.

Given that the Carver/Ford/Wolff school is perceived as belonging to a masculine tradition (and Ford in particular rarely brings women to the centre of his stories—*Wildlife*, his recent novella, is possibly the only piece of his fiction where a woman so much as shares the limelight), it is perhaps surprising that Wolff writes frequently, and very well, about women. The sympathy shown to both Mrs. Brooke and Ruth, Brooke's one-night stand, in 'An Episode in the Life of Professor Brooke', is repeated in several other of Wolff's tales; 'Face to Face' and 'In the Garden of the North American Martyrs' (which served as the title for the first collection in the U.S.) from *Hunters in the Snow* are both narratives told from a woman's point of view.

'Face to Face' exemplifies just how straightforward is Wolff's view of sexual relationships compared to the approach of his colleagues. The stories of Ford and Carver frequently feature marriages that have stretched beyond breaking-point, and one is left with the inescapable conclusion that these writers, despite their reputation for realism, look upon what happens between men and women as something peripheral to the lives of their (usually male) central characters. Carver's 'Menudo', for example, takes a commonplace romantic situation—the married narrator is in love with his neighbour, and is waiting for her to break the news of the affair to her husband—yet succeeds in making it strange and somehow otherworldly. At the story's conclusion the narrator is frantically sweeping the leaves off the garden of the house next door, watched by the perplexed couple who live there, and while the story is about all sorts of things (particularly, it seems to me, language), it does not focus on a relationship in the way that Wolff does in 'Face to Face' or 'Desert Breakdown 1968' (in *Back to the World*), or that Bobbie Ann Mason does in many of her stories. The confused marital set-up in 'Menudo' is used as a starting-point to examine other things.

'Face to Face' is the story of a relationship between a divorcee, Virginia, and Robert, a pathetically inadequate man that she meets through her neighbours. He is shy and polite, and is kind to Virginia's young son; but when the couple go away for the weekend for their first time alone together he shows himself to be almost frighteningly sexually repressed.

'It's bad sometimes, being alone', Virginia tells him sympathetically on their way back, after she has told him that she cannot continue with the relationship; 'Not to complain,' he replies. 'I do all right. It's different with men and women. The minute a woman gets alone she starts looking for someone.'[5] Virginia understands that this perceived difference is a fallacy ('So do men,' she tells Robert); Robert's tragedy is that whereas he thinks he is looking for sex without responsibility, as he understands that all men are, he is in effect looking for responsibility without sex, which frightens and disgusts him. His insistence on playing out a rôle that he has no interest in actually prevents him from achieving this wish.

The very first story in the collection, 'Next Door', contains an echo of Robert's unarticulated longing. The narrator appears to be sexually frustrated: his wife sleeps in a different bed, and stops his advances to her. Yet both he and his wife are appalled by the couple next door, not only because they mistreat their dog and their children, but more importantly because they find the physical demonstrativeness of their neighbours (they go into a passionate clinch against their fridge, where they are visible through the window) repulsive. 'My wife could hardly speak for a couple of hours afterwards. Later she said she would never waste her sympathy on that woman again.'[6] Despite the fact that the narrator seems to resent his wife's denial of his physical desire, the story ends with his strange and powerful description of an imaginary film that he would like to watch on TV:

> At the end we see the explorers sleeping in a meadow filled with white flowers. The blossoms are wet with dew and stick to their bodies . . . covering them completely, turning them white so that you cannot tell one from another, man from woman, woman from man.[7]

It is the kind of vision that Robert from 'Face to Face' would share if he had any kind of self-perception; its portrayal of a world where there is no gender difference has a particular resonance for men who find their sexual orientation difficult and painful.

Elsewhere in the stories Wolff presents a variety of women who are in many ways the victims of men. This, of course, hardly makes him a 'feminist' writer, according to accepted current notions of how women should be portrayed in fiction, but it is quite clear that the author is taking a position; it is hard for a man to read 'Face to Face' or 'Desert Breakdown 1968' without feeling a little uncomfortable. In the latter the central male character, hitch-hiking to pick up spare parts for his broken-down car, seriously contemplates leaving his German wife (only recently arrived in the U.S.) and son at a petrol station in the middle of nowhere. He is picked up by a bunch of hippies who have some location work on a film, and makes the decision to go with them, and changes his mind not because he feels any sense of duty but because the drugged driver of the car scares him.

'Sister', like 'Desert Breakdown', combines Wolff's contempt for the counter-culture with his sympathy for women mistreated by feckless men. The sister of the title is a young woman who attempts to befriend two men in a park, but who comes to understand that she attracts neither of them, and that consequently they have no interest in her. (The title comes from a reference to the fashionable '60s' greeting that the joint-smoking men use; in fact, these men have either a sexual interest in women or none at all, and this indication of brotherly feeling is hollow.)

The title of Wolff's second collection, *Back in the World*, is an expression that U.S. soldiers used in Vietnam (as is the title of Bobbie Ann Mason's novel *In Country*); Tobias Wolff actually saw active service in that war, and the fact that he spent the end of the '60s in South East Asia possibly explains why he seems to reserve a special venom for the drug culture. Never having been a part of the more positive aspects of the '60s, it is possible that he came back to observe only its unattractive addled rump. Apart from the men in 'Sister' and the hippies who pick up the narrator in 'Desert Breakdown, 1968', there is the pitiful coked-out foursome in 'Leviathan', and the sad figure of Bonnie in 'Passengers', as well as the incapable Donald in 'The Rich Brother'. Like much of Wolff's work, these stories have an angry, engaged edge to them that separates him from the other, cooler writers with whom he is often grouped.

Tobias Wolff

It is perhaps surprising that Wolff has not yet used his experiences in Vietnam in his writing. There is the occasional reference to the war: in 'Soldier's Joy', set on a barracks in the U.S.A., and in many ways a prototype for 'The Barracks Thief', Hooper remembers that in Vietnam

> We used to talk about how when we got back in the world we were going to do this and we were going to do that. Back in the world we were going to have it made. But ever since then it's been nothing but confusion.[8]

This is a sentiment that other characters in Wolff's fiction—Dave in 'The Poor Are Always With Us', for example, who crawled through gunfire to rescue his friends at Khe Sanh and now spends his days smoking pot and picking arguments—would identify with. Yet these allusions are infrequent, despite the wealth of material that Wolff presumably has to draw on.

What seem to interest him more are the masculine bonds that soldiering enforces, and 'The Barracks Thief' is in some ways a continuation of the exploration into masculinity that was begun in stories like 'Face to Face' and 'Sister'.

Like 'Hunters in the Snow' and 'Soldier's Joy', 'The Barracks Thief' (Wolff's longest work of fiction to date) centres around the relationship between three men, Bishop, Lewis and Hubbard, young soldiers waiting to be posted to Vietnam. They are wary of each other: they are regarded as outsiders by the other soldiers in the barracks, most of whom have already served in the war, and they know that to band together will only cement this exclusion. However, they are all sent out to guard an ammunition dump together, and a dangerous incident forms a bond between them. It is a brief friendship, because shortly afterwards Hubbard is attacked and has his wallet stolen while he is taking a shower, and Lewis, the least stable of the three, is revealed as the eponymous thief.

'The Barracks Thief' is narrated in both the first and third persons. The first-person narrator, Philip Bishop, is the furthest away of the trio from the central incidents of the story, in that he is neither robber or robbed; yet it is through him that Wolff can introduce the main themes of his novella. This, of course, is a standard use for a narrator, who is frequently an observer rather than a protagonist, but the prologue to the story, where we are told how Philip came to enlist, points towards Wolff's intentions here.

The first few pages are unusual, given the brevity of the novella and that Bishop is peripheral to the main action, in that they deal with first Philip's father, and how he came to leave his wife, and then Philip's relationship with his brother and his mother. The Bishops' story is in many ways an archetypal one: Guy Bishop, the father, adores his two sons yet leaves them for another woman. He hopes that this upheaval will not damage his relationship with the boys, but as Philip grows older he comes to despise him; Philip's brother Keith becomes withdrawn and incapable, and Philip starts to feel contempt for him too. Philip eventually enlists into the Army the morning after another incident with his father. (Keith, meanwhile, becomes a drop-out and disappears off to San Francisco. Hippies and soldiers, the author seems to be suggesting, can be two sides of the same coin.)

Wolff's decision to start the book with Guy Bishop and his family broadens the book's concerns; Philip is placed in a context outside the Army, and his inability to respond to his parents or his brother, or to form friendships, his placing himself in 'a family without women',[9] as one of the sergeants describes the barracks, is caused by his father's sexuality, indirectly at least. These inadequacies are set against Guy's recognition of his own love for his children:

> The worst fear he had was that by loving his children so much he was somehow endangering them, putting them in harm's way. At times he knew for a certainty that some fear was about to overtake them.[10]

Philip's mother is similarly self-aware; shortly after her husband walks out on her she is able to articulate her loss to herself:

> What had happened to them? Where were they? Where was her home, her cats, her garden? Where was the regard of her neighbours, the love of her family? Everything was gone.[11]

Philip, on the other hand, does not have these resources. When he attempts, in the middle of the night, to tell Keith to pull himself together, he finds himself shaking his brother but unable to say a word; when somebody dies on a training jump, Philip has to suppress the urge to giggle. He may not be crucial to the mechanics of the narrative, but he certainly belongs to Wolff's group of desperately unsympathetic narrators. It is hard to regard him simply as a pair of eyes.

In a way, Philip's shortcomings are focussed and exaggerated in the character of Lewis, the barracks thief. Lewis is a pitifully incapable young man with a very low I.Q. and a stunted, almost childlike understanding of what masculinity involves. He lies colourfully about his sexual experiences and needs (we later discover that he is a virgin), and when he is offered calamine lotion for a grotesquely poisoned hand he refuses by explaining simply that he is 'In the army'.[12] At one point in the story, Lewis finds the words 'liquor and women'[13] coming into his head unbidden when he is sitting in a bar: the corny, Wild West quality of these words seems to be an oblique hint that Lewis's version of what it is to be male is entirely second-hand.

His thieving is linked directly to his fear of failing as a man. The week before the events recounted in the story, Lewis refused a descent when he and his company had been practising rapelling from a 50' cliff. ('It wasn't the way you probably heard', he tells Bishop. 'I just didn't have the rope fixed right. I wasn't afraid.'[14]) The first sergeant calls him 'Tinkerbell' because of his cowardice, and when he hears this word again, in a cinema, there are crucial repercussions.

> Tinkerbell, Lewis says. When he hears the word his stomach clenches. He gets up and walks outside. . . . He takes the bottle of calamine lotion out of his pocket and throws it into the road. It shatters. I'm no Tinkerbell, he says. He watches the cars go by for a while, balling and unballing his fists, then turns and walks back into Fayetteville to find a girl.[15]

The girl that Lewis finds is a pathetic prostitute; he steals from his colleagues because he does not have enough money to pay her. Thus it is Lewis's warped sexuality, his crude machismo and fear of what he understands as effeminacy that provides the narrative's key event. (The breaking of the calamine bottle is obviously symbolic here, as Lewis was ambivalent about the use of the medication; the scene in which it is applied by a lonely school-teacher, incidentally, is given strong homo-erotic undertones.)

If Bishop and Lewis provide a troubling image of masculinity, the third of the trio of new recruits, Hubbard, is quietly balanced. He has no ambition to go to Vietnam and 'kill slopes'—'I shot a squirrel once and cried all night'[16]—and indeed we are told that he will become one of the Canadian deserters. Unlike Lewis and Bishop, he has friends, and when he learns that they have been killed in a car accident, his grief is genuine and appropriate. He is, however, an ineffectual figure, with none of Bishop's herd instincts (Bishop is quite prepared to take part in a ritual beating of Lewis after he has been revealed as the thief, even though in the end he finds he has no stomach for it) or Lewis's psychotic aggression (when Hubbard is attacked by Lewis during one of the thefts, he is left with a smashed nose). It would appear that the barracks has no real need or place for Hubbard's version of what constitutes maleness.

Possibly the single most powerful description in a very powerful novella is of Lafayetteville, the town nearest to the barracks:

> Recruits with shaved heads, as many as fifteen or twenty in a group, walk from bar to bar. . . . They fall silent when they come up to the clusters of prostitutes, but when they are well past they call things over their shoulders. . . . The lights are on over the bars, in the tattoo parlours and clothing stores, in the gadget shops that sell German helmets and Vietcong flags, Mexican throwing knives, lighters that look like pistols, exotic condoms, fireworks and dirty books.[17]

Tawdry sex and intimations of violence: the nightmarish vision of Lafayetteville that Wolff provides here is a summation of the world of 'The Barracks Thief'.

It is perhaps surprising, given Wolff's determination in the novella to strip away the more attractive myths surrounding masculinity, that he should cite Hemingway as an antecedent; after all, Hemingway is now ridiculed for his machismo, and is hardly remembered as a critic of the male psyche. Yet

Wolff has pointed out that in Hemingway's early work he managed to distance himself from notions that would engulf him later in his career. In an interview with Paul Ryan, Wolff expresses his admiration for Hemingway's first book, *In Our Time*:

> It's wonderfully tender . . . images of masculinity are held up very critically in that book. In 'Indian Camp', where the father and the uncle go to deliver this baby and they behave so brutally towards this woman, and the Indian kills himself while the baby's being born. . . . Now here's a man who's imprisoned in an idea of how he ought to behave in a situation . . . this is held up for close examination and it's very critical.

Wolff goes on to point out that later on in Hemingway's career

> you find him hardening his attitude and in a sense adopting the very stance which earlier on he was critical of . . . and it started getting into his work in a very unfortunate way. You get that kind of posturing in *Across the River and Into the Trees* and the later stuff . . . talking about who's got balls and all those things he does later. But, boy, that early work is tender.[18]

There is a similar tenderness in 'The Barracks Thief', although Wolff has to widen the book's scope to find it (in Guy's love for his sons, for example); if Wolff has borrowed from Hemingway, then it is from the early Hemingway, and there seems little danger now that the author of 'The Barracks Thief' will come to adopt any of the brutal masculinity he has so painstakingly and powerfully revealed to us, both in the novella and in many of the stories.

This Boy's Life, Wolff's most recent book, is a memoir of his extraordinary boyhood experiences. The model for the book, as Wolff has acknowledged, was Frank Conroy's *Stop Time*, which has unfortunately remained unpublished in the U.K.; both Conroy and Wolff use techniques usually associated with fiction than with autobiography (flashback, extensive and impossibly lengthy passages of dialogue, vivid characterization and an artfully disguised shaping of material) in order to examine childhoods that were bewilderingly full of emotional and physical upheaval.

Conroy's remarkable book is structurally more ambitious, in that it takes an almost cinematic liberty with its narrative. Key incidents switch the book backwards or forwards to a similarly crucial point in time (hence, presumably, the book's title), a device that Wolff uses rarely. And yet the two writers share an ability to be unflinchingly honest about their own youthful shortcomings and to avoid self-pity when looking back on experiences which would appear to allow plenty of scope for bitterness.

Conroy was born in 1936, nine years earlier than Wolff, and thus *Stop Time* and *This Boy's Life* are set at opposite ends of the '50s. The America that they describe, however, remains unchanged during that period; indeed, as seen through the eyes of the authors it is a country that has remained unchanged since the Depression of the '30s. In *The Grapes of Wrath* (1939) Steinbeck describes the hopeful migration to California of a group of dispossessed Oklahoma farmers. In *Stop Time* the young Conroy and his family (including stepfather Jean) travel down to Florida to become part of a workers' community, the brain-child of a socialist visionary who made small plots of land available for just a few dollars; in *This Boy's Life* Wolff and his mother travel from Florida to Utah, 'to get away from a man my mother was afraid of and to get rich on uranium'.[19] Both trips are inevitably doomed to failure: Jean can never make enough money to finish the house that he wishes to build, and by the time that mother and son arrive in Utah, they are too late, and the towns are swarming with unemployed people with a similar aim.

In a sense Wolff's journey is simply a continuation of Conroy's. Both families have dreams of transformation ('I didn't come to Utah to be the same boy I'd been before', Wolff writes [20]); and though it is important not to confuse the almost whimsical nature of the ways they seek to achieve it with the very real desperation of Steinbeck's Joads, these dreams have very strong antecedents in American literature, from Huck Finn onwards. Certainly the epic lengths of the journeys that take place in the two books (Conroy travels from Florida to New York and hitch-hikes down to Delaware, for example) remind us that in American fiction there has always been a promise inherent in the sheer size of the country.

Wolff also explains how his attempts to become a different boy involved a literal transformation: Tobias changes his name to Jack—after Jack London—thus tying himself firmly to a tradition that the form and theme of the book already hint at.

The two books have other incidental points of comparison: the way that the two boys are at the mercy of their mothers' love lives (in turn reminiscent of Richard Ford's teenage stories—the tone and setting of *This Boy's Life* in particular is markedly similar to Ford's work) is particularly noticeable. Whereas Conroy must learn to live with his mother's exotic, eccentric lover Jean, Wolff has to cope with first Roy (the man his mother was afraid of), who tracks the pair down in Utah, and then the extraordinary Dwight, a violent, mean-spirited bully.

Although it is quite clear that Wolff suffered considerably at the hands of Dwight, there are many incidents in the book which are presented with a self-condemnation reminiscent of the moral awareness shown in the stories. The opening scene exemplifies this approach: on the way to Utah the young Toby and his mother witness a horrific fatal accident in which a lorry plunges over the side of a cliff. Toby is aware that his mother has been very shaken by what they have seen:

> For the rest of the day she kept looking over at me, touching me, brushing back my hair. I saw the time was right to make a play for souvenirs. I knew she had no money for them, and I had tried not to ask, but now that her guard was down I couldn't help myself. When we pulled out of Grand Junction I owned a beaded Indian belt, beaded moccasins, and a bronze horse with a removable, tooled-leather saddle.[21]

There is a similar incident soon afterwards. Toby's mother is courted by a couple of young servicemen, who pretend to be horrified when they learn that the boy does not possess a bicycle, and seem to promise to do something about it. Later that night one of the men takes the mother out for the evening; when she returns, she is hysterical, for reasons both we and the narrator can only guess at, and Toby comforts her.

> In the morning we were shy with each other. I somehow managed not to ask her my question. That night I continued to master myself, but my self-mastery seemed like an act; I knew I was too weak to keep it up.
> My mother was reading.
> 'Mom?' I said.
> She looked up.
> 'What about the Raleigh?'
> She went back to her book without answering. I did not ask again.[22]

The dreadful honesty of these passages isolate characteristics common to most childhoods; just as in the fiction we are inveigled into sympathizing with the central character, only to find that we are identifying with someone at best morally ambiguous. Here is the boy in 'The Liar': one excruciating episode describes how Wolff carves some obscene graffiti in the school toilet, denies having done so, and protests his innocence to the extent that when his mother is called in by the headmaster to discuss the incident, she sides with the boy. The extraordinary and improbable end of the memoir sees Wolff lying his way in to a prestigious boarding-school by forging his school reports. ('I wrote without heat or hyperbole, in the words my teachers would have used if they had known me as I knew myself.'[23]) Even when he has achieved his goal, the falsification does not stop; when he receives a form from the school asking for his name as he wishes it to appear in the school catalogue, he writes 'Tobias Jonathan von Ansell-Wolff III'.[24]

Clarity requires some kind of balance, of course; and *This Boy's Life* is not simply a catalogue of self-loathing: Dwight's cruelties are presented unadorned, but with sufficient detail to recreate in the reader the manifest injustice of his behaviour. In the end, perhaps Wolff's most outstanding achievement in a memorable, moving and very funny book is that he has in effect turned himself into a fictional character, and writes with the affection, perspective and disbelief of a novelist.

'One of the many remarkable qualities of this writer's autobiography', Paul Bailey wrote in the *Sunday Times*, 'is the absence of the literary.'

> There are few references to books: Jack London is mentioned, and James Michener's *Hawaii*, and scouting manuals and comics, but there is nothing at all about the novelists and short-story writers who have influenced him.[25]

Carver, Ford, Wolff—these three share what is coming to look like an archetypal background for contemporary American literature. It is a background that seems to ensure a vitality of language and a variety of theme and character in the fiction of its owners; and it is a background which in England has no equivalent. Malcolm Bradbury has said that twentieth-century fiction belongs to the U.S., and if we want to look for an explanation as to why this should be so, perhaps it is here that we will find it.

NOTES

1. Tobias Wolff, *The Stories of Tobias Wolff* (Picador, 1988), pp. 51–2.
2. Unpublished interview, April 1988.
3. Wolff, *The Stories of Tobias Wolff*, p. 191.
4. Unpublished interview, April 1988.
5. Wolff, *The Stories of Tobias Wolff*, p. 82.
6. Ibid., p. 13.
7. Ibid., p. 15.
8. Ibid., p. 289.
9. Ibid., p. 409.
10. Ibid., p. 379.
11. Ibid., pp. 383–84.
12. Ibid., p. 415.
13. Ibid., p. 421.
14. Ibid., pp. 397–98.
15. Ibid., p. 419.
16. Ibid., p. 396.
17. Ibid., p. 418.
18. Unpublished interview, April 1988.
19. Tobias Wolff, *This Boy's Life* (Bloomsbury, 1989), p. 3.

20. Ibid., p. 7.
21. Ibid., p. 3.
22. Ibid., p. 46.
23. Ibid., pp. 180–81.
24. Ibid., p. 218.
25. *Sunday Times*, 30 April 1989.

8
André Dubus

André Dubus is an important minor writer. That is to say, it would be difficult to make a case for him to stand alongside Carver or Ford or Anne Tyler—his prose style is too inflexible, and his work lacks the resonance of these contemporaries—and yet his stories and novellas are worthy of attention, chiefly because of the devastating emotional impact that the best of them achieve.

There is no doubt that his cause has not been helped by some sloppy publishing in the U.K. His trilogy of novellas ('We Don't Live Here Anymore', 'Adultery', and 'Finding a Girl in America'), a sequence which contains his finest writing, were originally published with a fourth, unconnected, story and described as 'four linked novellas'; when this book was withdrawn and replaced by *The Collected Stories of André Dubus*, only the central tale in the trilogy was printed in the collection. It is thus currently difficult for British readers to be able to make an informed judgement on Dubus's work, but any study of it must begin with an examination of the powerful trilogy, which dissects the emotional lives of two couples, Jack Linhart (the narrator of the story) and his wife Terry, and Hank and Edith Allison.

Like many of Dubus's characters, these four are markedly and refreshingly different from the inarticulate, unaware types that populate so much of contemporary American literature (both Jack and Hank are teachers, and Hank has ambitions as a writer), and much of their dialogue consists of direct, perceptive analyses of their emotional problems, insight upon insight. This does not, however, result in any dissipation of tension; the insights are invariably conflicting, and in any case the situations that the characters frequently find themselves in are quite often too painful, too serious, to be eased by any amount of self-knowledge.

'We Don't Live Here Anymore', the first of the three, introduces with bewildering rapidity the complicated emotional currents that run between the two couples. As Edith and Jack visit a liquor store to buy beer at the very beginning of the story, it becomes apparent that they are having an adulterous relationship; within four pages Terry is hurling a glass at Jack's head. In many ways the content of 'We Don't Live Here Anymore' is resolutely banal: Terry eventually gets drawn into a relationship with Hank, against her better judgement, and despite Jack's very real feelings for Edith, he decides ultimately that his place is with his wife and two children. What separates the story from soap opera is the author's bleak refusal to sentimentalize his material, and the quality of his insights into the state of marriage in the last quarter of the twentieth century.

Occasionally it would appear to be the institution of marriage itself which is responsible for the problems that beset the central characters. 'For some years now I have been spiritually allergic to the words husband and wife', says Jack.

> When I read or hear husband I see a grimly serene man in a station wagon; he is driving his loud family on a Sunday afternoon. . . . When someone says wife I see the confident, possessive and amused face of a woman in her kitchen. . . . She is wearing a new dress. From her scheming heart his balls hang like a trophy taken in battle from a young hero long dead.[1]

There are elements of this portrait—the 'possessive', 'scheming' woman, the castrated man—that suggest a clichéd misogyny and an outmoded, self-pitying machismo. The latter quality in particular is frequently visible in the words and actions of the two central male characters. When Jack and Hank visit a bar for a beer one evening, Hank is fascinated by the behaviour of one of the other customers, a middle-aged man having a quick drink before returning home to prepare dinner for his wife. Hank buys him a drink, and the man expresses his desire to 'some day come in here and get me one of those fish platters'.² When Hank and Jack leave the bar, Hank leaves enough money to cover the customer's long-coveted dinner.

It is an obscure gesture, only illuminated later when Hank and Jack relate the story to Edith. 'Hank, that was cruel', his wife tells him. 'I know, but he had no balls. Cooking, for Christ sake.'³ Castration again: these young men would appear to be developing something of a complex. It can come as something of a shock for the modern reader to confront these unreconstructed masculine attitudes to sexual rôles; yet after the aggressively masculine world of Richard Ford, and the curiously sexless stories of Raymond Carver, Dubus's characters are intriguing.

The friendship between Hank and Jack is of the standard jogging-and-drinking variety, but the differences between the two men are interesting, and Dubus contrasts the friends effectively. Hank has long since given up on monogamy as a workable ethic, and yet paradoxically his marriage would appear to be in better shape than Jack's:

> His marriage wasn't a grave because Hank wasn't dead; he used his marriage as a center and he moved out from it on azimuths of madness and when he was tired he came back.⁴

Jack, on the other hand, is new to the deceptions and dangers of adultery, preferring to believe for as long as he could that his relationship with his wife was adequate and durable. Before Hank is aware that his friend and his wife are having an affair, he scorns his friend's struggle: 'You're nineteenth century, Jack', he tells him.

> 'It's why you've been faithful so long. Your conscience is made for whores but you're too good for that, so you end up worse: monogamous.'
> 'What's this made for whores shit?'
> 'The way it used to be. Man had his wife and kids. That was one life. And he had his whore. He knew which was which, see; he didn't get them confused. But now it's not that way: a man has a wife and a girlfriend and they get blurred, you see, he doesn't know where his emotional deposits are supposed to be. . . . He does something stupid: either he breaks with

the girl and tries to love only his wife, or he leaves his wife and marries the girl. . . .'[5]

Either option, according to Hank, is a disaster; if he leaves the wife, 'he'll be in the same shit in a few years'; a monogamous relationship with the wife has already failed, so pointless to try again. In 'We Don't Live Here Anymore' Hank's ideas are presented as tenable: Edith readjusts in order to accommodate them (we are told at the end of the book that she has taken another lover to replace Jack). 'It's not love', she tells Jack. 'It's marriage. We have a good home. We respect each other. There's affection.'[6]

Jack's decision to return to his wife, and to attempt to remain monogamous, leave him and his wife with something similar—respect and affection—but without the prospect, for Jack at least, of any real passion for the remainder of his life:

> . . . and I felt my life was out of my hands, that I must now play at a ritual of mortality and goodbye, the goodbye not only to Edith but to love itself, for I would never again lie naked with a woman I loved. . . .[7]

It is a bleak future, bleakly and powerfully imagined and articulated, and it is passages such as these that make Dubus worth reading.

If one strand of 'We Don't Live Here Anymore' presents arguments for and against adultery and fidelity, the other is a portrayal of a modern American woman's lot. What is interesting about the presentation of Terry is that it is essentially phenomenological; that is to say, Dubus resists the temptation to tinker with it so that it is ideologically 'correct' but fundamentally unrepresentative of her lot. Terry is a housewife, pure and simple—and not only that, she is an inept one. Much of Jack's resentment towards his wife stems from this ineptitude: he discovers that his children are sleeping in sheets that had been soaked in urine and allowed to dry unwashed, that unwashed pots are left in forgotten corners of the house until they are coated in mould. (Like many of his contemporaries, Dubus is a writer obsessed by surfaces and physical characteristics, although he is alone in exploring their resonances and metaphors.

At one point, Jack recalls how 'newly married one morning [Terry] was holding a can of frozen orange juice over a pitcher and the sound of its slow descent drove us back to bed'.[8])

When Jack and Terry watch a production of *Uncle Vanya* on television, Dr. Astrov's lines—'She is beautiful, there's no denying that, but. . . . You know she does nothing but eat, sleep, walk about, fascinate us all by her beauty—nothing more. . . . And an idle life cannot be pure'—make Jack want to glance at his wife.

Despite Jack's raging, Terry remains a sharply sympathetic character: rootless, utterly dependent on her husband, without the shaping and succouring discipline of work. The most powerful and overwhelmingly affecting section of the novella comes when Dubus allows Terry her own voice, and in a long section of dialogue she sets about trying to articulate to her husband exactly what her marriage has left her with:

> How would you know if you hate me? You don't even know me. You say, 'You are what you do.' But do you really believe that? Does that mean I'm a cook, an errand runner, a fucker, a bed maker, and on and on . . . a goddamn *cleani*ng woman, for Christ sake? If you . . . *you*, you bastard . . . lost all discipline, just folded up and turned drunk and was fired, *I'd* love you, and I'd get a job and support us too. Maybe no-one else would love you. . . . So what is it that I love? If action doesn't matter. I love you . . . I love Jack Linhart. And I say you're more than what you do.[9]

This speech is at the heart of the trilogy, because all three of the stories feature women (Edith in 'Adultery', Lori in 'Finding a Girl in America') whose understanding of the love between men and women is wiser, more mature than that of the men. It is archetypal Dubus dialogue—impassioned, perceptive, colloquially articulate, raw—and a perfect example of how, when most contemporary American writing depends on the inability to express for its emotional effect, Dubus bravely relies on the quality of his perceptions.

It is at the end of Terry's diatribe that Jack announces to her that he loves Edith, a shattering *coup de théâtre* (and in many ways Dubus's skills are really those of a dramatist) that leaves her a truly pitiable figure. (It should be pointed out that Dubus's use of a first-person narrator is really more complex than it appears; despite Jack's self-justifications, and the lack of another viewpoint, Terry's desolation here is nonetheless real and extraordinarily painful.) 'We Don't Live Here Anymore' may be narrated by a man, but it is an extremely effective account of the destruction of a woman.

Given the routine infidelities and betrayals that stud the first novella, the title of its sequel, 'Adultery', is somewhat ironic. The story combines the themes of the first, this time from Edith's perspective (although 'Adultery' is narrated in the third person), with another of Dubus's concerns, the Catholic church, which features strongly in another Dubus novella, the brilliant 'Voices from the Moon'.

'Adultery' takes place a couple of years after the events described in 'We Don't Live Here Any More'. Both couples remain married, in the fashion arrived at in the first story: Edith and Hank are still using their marriage as 'a center' from which they travel out; Jack's experiment with alternative partners is over:

> He did not love Terry but he could not hurt her, nor leave his children, and he was faithful now, he drank too much, and often he talked with long and embittered anger about things of no importance.[10]

Jack and Terry are minor characters here, however: 'Adultery' is the story of Edith's affair with Joe, an ex-priest mortally ill with cancer. It is, inevitably, an unbearably painful narrative (hence the bitter irony of the moralizing title), yet its purpose, thankfully, is not simply to anatomize a relationship that will end with a premature death.

Dubus begins the story with a quotation from Simone Weil, '... love is a direction and not a state of the soul', and there is indeed a progression, an emotional journey, in 'Adultery'. It is Edith's journey, away from the simplicity of a life in which a woman loves her husband and is loved in return, and if

Joe's death has any figurative meaning then it would seem to emphasize the naïveté of this desire, as it marks the end of a stage in Edith's emotional development.

The first section of 'Adultery' deals with the details of Joe's illness, and the mechanics of Edith's current relationship with Hank; the second section furnishes us with details of Edith's marriage. 'All she had ever wanted to be was a nice girl someone would want to marry',[11] it begins, and given the emotional detritus that Dubus has strewn over the preceding pages and the previous novella, the uncomplicated nature of this desire is heartbreaking (if, once again, unlikely to endear the author to a certain brand of feminist). Dubus goes on to plot the history of Hank and Edith, from the early unplanned conception of their daughter Sharon to Hank's first affair with a French woman and its powerfully malign effect on Edith's love for her husband:

> . . . it was harmony she had lost. Until now her marriage had been a circle, like its gold symbol on her finger. Wherever she went she was still inside it. It had a safe, gentle circumference, and mortality and the other perils lay outside of it.[12]

Edith attempts to replace the harmony she has lost with a different kind of faith:

> She wanted to fall in love with God. She wanted His fingers to touch her days, to restore meaning to those simple tasks which now drained her spirit. . . . But she knew it was no use: she had belief, but not faith: she could not bring God under her roof and into her life. He awaited her death.[13]

It is perhaps unsurprising, then, that her final adulterous relationship should be with a man who has come to a similar conclusion. (After Joe has left the Church—not because of Edith, but because of the need for someone like her—he continues to attend daily mass but no longer receives Communion. 'It was not that he believed he was sinning with her; it was that he didn't know.'[14]) For Joe and Edith, Weil's 'direction' is away from one kind of simple certitude to another, more complex (but more tenable) variety. Joe's imminent death enables Edith to resolve to divorce Hank. 'It's because he's dying, yes', she tells her husband. 'But you're dying too. I can feel it in your chest just like I could feel it when I rubbed him when he hurt.'[15] It is a decision that causes her greater pain than the prospect of her lover's imminent death: she is 'feeling . . . a grief that will last, she knows, longer than her grieving for Joe'.[16]

Of the four adulterers in 'We Don't Live Here Anymore', only Hank now remains wedded, as it were, to the idea that a monogamous marital relationship is impossible. Jack and Terry have decided that their imperfect union is ultimately less harmful, if unsatisfying; Edith has now realized that her husband's lack of fidelity is something she can no longer tolerate. Hank has remained a problematic character throughout the two stories: unbearably smug (in his criticism of Jack, for example), overbearingly macho, deceitful, selfish. Never particularly sympathetic, his attempts to make love with Edith shortly before Joe's death are particularly repugnant. The final part of the trilogy, 'Finding a Girl in America', is remarkable in that Dubus sets out to complete the square by placing Hank at the centre of the story and according him the same understanding previously shown to the other three central characters.

Dubus's approach in 'Finding a Girl in America' verges on the formulaic; just as in the other two novellas the reader is immediately immersed in a complicated and emotive scenario (Jack's adultery with Edith in the first, Joe's illness in the second), so in the third Hank learns from his new young lover (one of his students) that his previous lover aborted his child. He reacts by vomiting, a physical response entirely in keeping with the intense physicality of the novella's first few pages, which describe a meal, a bout of love-making and even the toiletry habits of Hank and Lori (the new lover). Hank's violent reaction to Monica's abortion is hardly likely to gain much sympathy from those readers unsure of how to respond to his previous behaviour; after all, his history of promiscuity is an unpromising indication of his suitability for fatherhood. It is difficult to detect any ironic narrative detachment on the author's part, however, and one's suspicions here are that it is only a '70s' 'Me Decade' male that will be able to respond empathetically to Hank's plight (it is interesting, therefore, that Dubus's books carry ringing endorsements from *Playboy* magazine and from John Updike, whose work is perhaps the closest in theme to Dubus's own).

In fact, it is the abortion that is instrumental in Hank's realization that his old life-style is no longer what he wants; and just as importantly, he can no longer make a case for it emotionally or intellectually:

> He said Jack was right. The country had gone fucking crazy. He said I'll bet ninety percent of abortions are because somebody's making love with somebody they shouldn't. So were too many people. So had he, for too long. But no more. Things were screwed up and the women had lost again. A sexual revolution and a liberation movement and look what it got them.[17]

It is an understanding that dates the novella, not because of the reference to the sexual revolution, but because an articulate, thoughtful man has taken so long to arrive at this conclusion; nevertheless it has a powerful emotional thrust to it, especially when allied to some of the perceptions that Hank has about his marriage to Edith ('She had not made him leave her life because he was unfaithful; she made him leave because she was; because he had changed her'[18]) and to his feelings for and relationship with Lori.

In many ways, the character of Lori is unmistakeably the creation of a male product of the 1960s: she is sensitive, beautiful, nubile and perceptive beyond her tender years, and many women might argue that she is the stuff of male fantasy. Certainly Hank expects a lot from the young girls that he seduces, and his anger at Monica's unilateral decision to terminate her pregnancy is indefensible. Yet although women may object to much of Dubus's *modus operandi* here, it should be pointed out that Lori's understanding of her own sexuality, and an understanding of the nature of love that rivals that of Terry and Edith, provides the story's emotional centre. Given that the story was written some ten years before the advent of AIDS, Lori's wisdom is remarkably prescient (such sentiments are more in keeping with current mores):

Already two lovers and she wished she could cancel the first and, if she and Hank broke up, there would be a third and she would be going the way of her sisters who had recovered, she thought, too many times from too many lovers, were growing tougher, she thought, from repeated pain; were growing, she thought, cynical; and when they visited home, they talked about love but never permanent love anymore . . . she knew what they needed was marriage.[19]

Lori has come to the same conclusion as Hank, but it has taken the man some fifteen years longer to get there; it is entirely logical, and overwhelmingly moving, that at the trilogy's epiphanic close, Hank and Lori should vow to marry.

I began this chapter by saying that Dubus was an important minor writer. I do not wish to negate the emotional force of these three stories, yet they contain some of the flaws which seem to me to support this assertion, and they are flaws that have an importance and a resonance beyond the trilogy itself. I am not referring here to the over-complex tumble of conjunctions which constitutes a typical Dubus sentence, although his prose does lack the variety of Ford's, and the simplicity of Carver's. But there is an insistence on a shared culture in these three stories which has marred several other recent interesting American novels (Anne Lamott's *Rosie* is an example that springs to mind), and it is an insistence that is in itself interesting.

Elsewhere I have discussed how Bobbie Ann Mason has used brand names and other cultural peripherals in order to furnish and colour the world of her characters. Thus one can find references to *M.A.S.H.* and to the Beatles and countless other programmes and songs and show-business celebrities. Similarly in Dubus's trilogy of novellas one can find Judy Collins and Bob Dylan and Cannonball Adderley and Crosby Stills Nash and Young; one can also find Chekhov (on more than one occasion) and Conrad. There is a difference in the way these two writers utilize these cultural touchstones, however.

Firstly it should be pointed out that Dubus's pop cultural references have their source to a large extent in the counter-culture of the '60s and early '70s, a movement that was essentially middle-class in its character. Whereas any American will instantly identify Mason's references, which she uses non-pejoratively in order to place a character (it is not necessary to be a Johnny Carson fan in order to understand what he is doing in a story), Dubus's names will only really have relevance to a certain age and class, especially as he uses them in a way which demands a shared appreciation of the merits of these cultural icons. Thus, Hank and Bob Dylan: '. . . and he listened to Dylan, the angry songs about women'; '. . . and with Dylan's hurt and angry encouragement. . .'; 'he listened to "Just Like a Woman" and thought, *Maybe that's what I was doing*. . . .'[20] Similarly, Edith and Judy Collins: 'She saw Judy as a small bird singing on a wire. . . .'[21] And Lori and Chekhov: '. . . she had no way of knowing whether tonight's understanding . . . came from reading Chekhov.'[22]

At the climax of Frederick Exley's strange but brilliant 1968 book *A Fan's Notes*, the narrator (who may or may not be the real Frederick Exley) arrives at an unwanted state of self-knowledge, moments after he has involved himself in a useless and damaging fist-fight:

> I fought because I understood, and could not bear to understand, that it was my destiny—unlike that of my father, whose fate it was to hear the roar of the crowd—to sit in the stands and acclaim others. It was my fate, my destiny, my end, to be a fan.[23]

There is a sense in which this is true of Dubus. His continued use in the trilogy of what are patently sources of inspiration arguably relegates him to fan status, not simply because of the references to these sources, but because they are on occasions required to do the author's work for him: Dylan and Chekhov are presumed to trigger a response in the reader that suggests there is a cultural hegemony in operation here.

'Voices from the Moon' is Dubus's strongest piece of work in part because the class and education of the characters prevent the same kind of utilization of these cultural triggers. There are plenty of names to be found nonetheless: Zola, Kate Chopin, Jean Rhys, de Maupassant, Colette, Schubert,

Mozart, Beethoven, Tchaikovsky, Bach, Scarlatti, Schumann, the other Chopin, Debussy, Billie Holiday, Ella Fitzgerald, Brubeck, Ellington, Charlie Parker, Coltrane and Sarah Vaughan . . . all in the same paragraph. It is difficult to see the purpose of such a list, particularly as it hardly assists the reader in imagining the character with such stifling and relatively commonplace good taste. Unlike Chekhov in 'Finding a Girl in America', however, these characters are not asked to carry any thematic weight, and their inclusion is indicative merely of Dubus's endearing and enduring status as a consumer of the arts.

The novella is another example of Dubus's continued interest in extreme emotional situations, and yet again we are thrust into the story at its point of crisis. Richie, the young boy at the centre of 'Voices from the Moon', has overheard his father and his older brother Larry arguing; it becomes apparent that Greg, the father, wants to marry his son's ex-wife Brenda. Dubus quickly throws in two more elements: Richie's love for the Catholic church and his ambition to join the seminary, and the story of the perverse sexual relationship between Larry and Brenda which eventually destroyed their marriage.

It is ostensibly an absurdly melodramatic set-up, but the writer's method of beginning the story at an emotional climax precludes sensationalism; quite simply, there are no sensations. It is patently clear that Dubus wants to examine reactions rather than produce revelations, and this bizarrely complicated family provides rich pickings. There is a question here that echoes through much of Dubus's work—how does one tolerate a situation that is intolerable?—and many of his characters have to learn that it is a question to which there is no answer. 'We don't have to live great lives, we just have to understand and survive the ones we've got',[24] Larry's mother tells him at the story's conclusion, and it is a line crucial to an understanding of this author's fiction.

'Voices from the Moon' is above all about physicality. 'Flesh is Dubus's subject', wrote Peter Kemp in his review of *Selected Stories* in the *Sunday Times*. 'Its pleasures, pains, strengths and vulnerabilities are palpable everywhere.'[25] Its pleasures and strengths are here reserved more or less entirely for the young: Richie's joyful love of sports, his delight in the scents of his friend Melissa. And his love for God and for the Mass is physical and touchingly literal: 'Now Father Oberti lifted the chalice and Richie imagined being inside of him, feeling what he felt as the wine he held became the blood of Christ.'[26] 'You believe it's God? The bread and wine?', he asks Melissa while attempting to explain why he attends Mass every day. 'Yes.' 'That's what I mean. It's God, so how can I stay home. When He's there every day . . . I love it. It's better than anything. The feeling.'[27] For the adults, the flesh is a source of danger and darkness. Greg's physical relationship with Brenda has necessitated a painful turn in his relationship with his son; meanwhile, Brenda and Larry have learnt that to act on desires, to make them physical, is perilously foolhardy. (Larry and Brenda have enacted a kind of voyeuristic troilism; they picked up single men from bars, invited them back to their flat, and when Larry went to bed pleading drunkenness, Brenda would seduce the man in the living room while Larry waited for her in the bedroom.) The story's obsession with sensuality is underlined by an overwhelming number of descriptions of physical sensations: tastes (of cigarettes, breakfast, alcohol), smells, feelings. Parental and fraternal love and concern is physical; Richie recalls how, when he returned home bloody from a beating by two older boys, Greg and Larry rushed from the house, found the bullies and slapped them until 'they fell and crawled away in the dirt, crying.'[28] Even Greg's job—he owns two ice-cream parlours—is a link between the pleasures of youth and the painful duty of adulthood.

Richie is becoming old enough to know that his life, and the pleasure he takes in it, is about to become complicated by his desires, just as his family's lives have been. In a reverie it comes to him that his life must consist of love for his family, despite the difficulties they are causing him:

> He had to love them all, and he could do that only with Christ, and to receive Christ he could not love Melissa. He knew that from her scents this morning, and her voice, and her kiss.[29]

It is a Catholic struggle, between the flesh and the Devil, and an echo of the battle that Brenda and Larry have already fought and lost; and though it is, of course, adolescent, unthreatening, Dubus places it at the heart of 'Voices from the Moon' because Richie eventually learns the value of compromise, and the wisdom of redrawing lines to deal with a narrowing of options. The last chapter of the story is devoted to the boy, and his recognition that his fight against his desire for Melissa is one that he cannot and possibly should not win:

> He was watching her mouth, and he swallowed, and he knew he was lost. If only he could be lost without fear. If only his heart could keep growing larger and larger until he knew he had to hold her.[30]

The story ends with Richie lying with Melissa on the grass, and therefore from one angle with a kind of defeat; yet it is an upbeat ending, because the boy has learnt quickly and easily which fights he is capable of winning. He has abandoned himself to his love for the girl, but ultimately he is aware that this will not exclude his love for God, and that the two will simply have to learn to co-exist, just as his mother has predicted that Larry will learn to live with the rearrangements in his own personal life. Neither of them, Dubus seems to be saying, will live good lives; but they will survive and understand the lives that they have got.

It is a theme that runs through much of Dubus's short stories, although the necessary compromises are not always so benign. In 'Killings', a father whose son has been murdered realizes that he will only ever be able to purchase any kind of peace by murdering his son's killer. It is a terrifying tale, not least because Matt, the father, is as recognizably decent and thoughtful as so many of the author's characters; thus an identification is forged between murderer and reader.

Dubus's fascination with the physical world and its banal ability to affect relationships is similarly repeated elsewhere; in 'The Winter Father', which deals yet again with separation, the central character comes to realize that the quality of his contact with his children is altered by the seasons:

> ... in summer he and his children were as he had yearned for them to be in winter: they were no longer confined to car or buildings to remind them why they were there. The long beach and the sea were their lawn; the blanket their home; the ice chest and thermos their kitchen. They lived as a family again.[31]

André Dubus

In many ways it is an emotional territory that has been abandoned by contemporary fiction, mostly because at its worst this kind of writing can resemble sentimental middle-brow television drama (cf. *thirtysomething*). It is important, however, that writers such as Dubus continue to retain a foothold in this area; contemporary relationships are simply too complex to be dealt with competently in fifty-minute chunks punctuated by advertisements. Dubus has made it his task to reveal with 'a luminous delicacy' (John Updike's memorable phrase) how and why things that happen between people go wrong and, occasionally, go right.

NOTES

1. André Dubus, *We Don't Live Here Anymore* (Picador, 1984), p. 117.
2. Ibid., p. 97.
3. Ibid., p. 102.
4. Ibid., p. 118.
5. Ibid., p. 98.
6. Ibid., p. 153.
7. Ibid., p. 151.
8. Ibid., p. 107.
9. Ibid., p. 138.
10. Ibid., p. 191.
11. Ibid., p. 167.
12. Ibid., p. 183.
13. Ibid., p. 183.
14. Ibid., p. 202.
15. Ibid., p. 211.
16. Ibid., p. 213.
17. Ibid., p. 274.
18. Ibid., p. 232.
19. Ibid., p. 273.
20. Ibid., pp. 225–27.
21. Ibid., p. 184.
22. Ibid., p. 272.
23. Frederick Exley, *A Fan's Notes* (Penguin, 1990), p. 326.
24. André Dubus, *Selected Stories* (Picador, 1990), p. 355.
25. *Sunday Times*, 11 March 1990.
26. *Selected Stories*, pp. 291–92.
27. Ibid., p. 296.
28. Ibid., p. 311.
29. Ibid., p. 338.
30. Ibid., p. 357.
31. Ibid., p. 39.

Index

Across the River and Into the Trees (Hemingway), 145
Allen, Woody, 17
Amis, Kingsley, 11, 33
Amis, Martin, 33
Apple, Max, 117
Applefield, David, 30
Austen, Jane, 8, 79

Bailey, Paul, 149
Baker, Nicholson, 27
Balzac, Honoré de, 90–1
Barstow, Stan, 33
Barth, John, 90, 116, 124
Barthelme, Donald, 124
Beatles, the, 85–6, 160
Beattie, Ann, 7–10, 11, 27, 72; 'In the White Night', 8, 9–10; 'Janus', 8, 9; *Love Always*, 8; *Picturing Will*, 8; 'Skeletons', 8–9
Beckett, Samuel, 40, 129
Bellow, Saul, 79
Bonfire of the Vanities (Wolfe), 54, 91
Bowles, Paul, 137
Bradbury, Malcolm, 33, 149
Braine, John, 33
Bright Lights, Big City (McInerney), 12, 15, 54
Buford, Bill, 9, 10, 12, 33–4
Burroughs, William, 119
Byatt, A. S., 18, 19, 20

Camus, Albert, 101
Carson, Johnny, 161
Carver, Raymond, 9, 20, 27, 30–51, 54, 74, 75, 80, 93, 116, 125, 133, 134, 138, 149, 151, 153, 160; 'The bath', 38, 40–2, 43; 'Bicycles, muscles, cigarets', 35–6; 'Blackbird Pie', 47–8; *Cathedral*, 33, 42–4, 46; 'Cathedral', 44, 49; 'Collectors', 35; 'Distance', 38–9; *Elephant*, 33, 45–50; 'Elephant', 49; 'Errand', 45, 48, 49–50; 'Everything stuck to him', 38–9; 'The Father', 48; 'Fever', 43–4; *Fires*, 38, 39; 'Fires', 31–2, 43; 'Gazebo', 37–40; 'Gravy', 51; 'How about this?' 37; 'Intimacy', 46–7; 'Menudo', 138; 'Mr. Coffee and Mr. Fixit', 39–40; *A New Path to the Waterfall*, 50; 'Night School', 34–5; 'Put yourself in my shoes', 46; 'A small, good thing', 9, 38, 40–2, 43, 44, 50; 'The student's wife', 45; 'The third thing that killed my father off', 37; 'Viewfinder', 37, 40; *Where I'm Calling From*, 33, 45; 'Where is everyone?', 40; *What We Talk About When We Talk About Love*, 33, 37–43; 'Why don't you dance?', 37; *Will You Please Be Quiet, Please*, 33, 34, 46, 48
Cather, Willa, 76, 77
Caulfield, Holden, 105
Cheever, John, 27, 45, 133, 137
Chekhov, Anton, 32, 45, 133, 137
Collins, Judy, 160–61
Conroy, Frank, 146–47
'Conversation with my Father, A' (Paley), 19–20

Day, Doris, 121, 122
Dean, James, 34
Diner, 53, 54
Drabble, Margaret, 33
Dubus, André, 151–65; 'Adultery', 151, 155, 156–58; 'Finding a Girl in America', 151, 155, 158–61; 'Killings', 164; 'Voices from the Moon', 156, 162–64; 'We Don't Live Here Anymore', 151, 152–56, 158; 'The Winter Father', 164
Dylan, Bob, 160–61

Easton Ellis, Bret, 13
Erdich, Louise, 30
Esquire, 30
L'Étranger (Camus), 101

Index

Everything that Rises Must Converge (O'Connor), 75
Exley, Frederick, 161

A Fan's Notes (Exley), 161
Faulkner, William, 94, 120
Ford, Richard, 9, 10, 27, 31, 33, 45, 54, 80, 90, 125, 133, 134, 138, 149, 151, 153, 160; 'Children', 105; 'Communist', 105; 'Empire', 108; 'Going to the Dogs', 108, 109–10; 'Great Falls', 105, 108; 'Optimists', 105, 106–8, 109, 112; *A Piece of My Heart*, 93, 94–7, 100; *Rock Springs*, 105–10, 111, 113; 'Rock Springs', 108, 109; *The Sportswriter*, 42, 70–1, 72, 93, 95, 97–105, 106, 108, 109; 'Sweethearts', 108; *The Ultimate Good Luck*, 97; *Wildlife*, 105–6, 110–13, 138

Gallagher, Tess, 45, 50
Granta, 9, 10, 11, 33, 74, 89, 93, 116, 124, 133
Guardian, 45
Gramsci, Antonio, 119
Grapes of Wrath, The (Steinbeck), 146

Hairspray, 53, 54
Hannah, Barry, 117
Harrison, Jim, 54
Helprin, Mark, 30–1, 35–6
Hemingway, Ernest, 32, 40, 45, 116, 144–45
Henry, O., 133
Hopper, Edward, 34
Horse Crazy (Indiana), 13
Housebreaker of Shady Hill, The (Cheever), 137

Indiana, Gary, 13
'Indian Camp' (Hemingway), 145
In Our Time (Hemingway), 145

James, Henry, 79
Janowitz, Tama, 7, 12, 13–16, 25, 54; 'Kurt and Natasha, a Relationship', 16; 'Modern Saint #271', 14; 'Patterns', 15; 'The Slaves in New York', 15; *Slaves of New York*, 13–16; 'You and the Boss', 16
Johnson, Diane, 53, 76–7, 79, 87, 88, 105

Karbo, Karen, 13

Keillor, Garrison, 75
Kemp, Peter, 162
Kerouac, Jack, 119
Kesey, Ken, 119

Lamott, Anne, 160
Leavitt, David, 27–8
Lee, Hermione, 75
Lehmann-Haupt, Christopher, 34
Levin, Bernard, 94
Levinson, Barry, 53
Lish, Gordon, 117
Little Women (Alcott), 88
Lively, Penelope, 11
Lodge, David, 33
London, Jack, 147

McInerney, Jay, 12–13
M.A.S.H., 86, 87, 160
Mason, Bobbie Ann, 7, 12, 31, 33, 53, 54, 72, 74–91, 113, 116, 137, 160–61; 'Airwaves', 82–4; 'Coyotes', 84–5; *In Country*, 12, 76, 85–9, 105, 140; *Love Life*, 74, 81, 82–5; 'Lying Doggo', 89; 'Nancy Culpepper', 89; 'A New Wave Format', 81; 'The Rookers', 80–1; *Shiloh*, 77–81, 89; 'Shiloh', 77–80, 83; 'Still Life with Watermelon', 81–2
Michener, James, 149
Minot, Susan, 13
Moore, Lorrie, 7, 12, 13, 87; 'Amahl and the Night Visitors', 19; *Anagrams*, 21; 'How', 17; 'How to Be an Other Woman', 17–18, 19, 20; 'How to Become a Writer', 17; 'How to Talk to Your Mother (Notes)', 17, 18; 'The Jewish Hunter', 25–7; 'The Kids' Guide to Divorce', 17; *Like Life*, 22–7; 'Like Life', 22–3; 'To Fill', 20–1; *Self-Help*, 16–22, 23; 'Two Boys', 22–4; 'Vissi D'Arte', 24; 'What is Seized', 21–2; 'You're Ugly, Too', 25
Moviegoer, The (Percy), 97
Murdoch, Iris, 33

Nabokov, Vladimir, 89
Nelson, Willie, 89
New Yorker, 7, 9, 11, 72, 78, 117
New York Review of Books, 76
New York Times, 34, 76

Oates, Joyce Carol, 117

O'Connor, Flannery, 75, 76, 77, 94, 136
O'Hara, John, 133
On the Beach, 117
O! Pioneers (Cather), 76

Paley, Grace, 18–20
Peck, Gregory, 117
Percy, Walker, 75, 97, 105
Phillips, Jayne Ann, 116–24, 125, 131; *Black Tickets*, 116–21, 123; 'Black Tickets', 119; 'Blue Moon', 122–24; 'El Paso', 119, 120–21; *Fast Lanes*, 121–22; 'Home', 117–19, 121; 'Lechery', 119; 'Souvenir', 119; 'Strangers in the Night', 119; 'Wedding Picture', 117, 123
Pinter, Harold, 45
Playboy, 159
Pritchett, V. S., 45
Pynchon, Thomas, 90

Reagan, Ronald, 34, 88, 104–5
Rhoda, 17
Rosie (Lamott), 160
Rushdie, Salman, 45
Ryan, Paul, 135, 145

Sage, Lorna, 94
Sexton, David, 31, 37, 40
Shaphard, Robert, 117
Sillitoe, Alan, 33
Smartt Bell, Madison, 7
Spillane, Mickey, 93, 97
Spin, 16
Springsteen, Bruce, 16, 87, 131
Steinbeck, John, 35, 146
Stop Time (Conroy), 145–47
Sudden Fiction, 117
Sunday Times, 94, 149, 162

Talking Heads, 87
Tallent, Elizabeth, 7, 10–12, 27, 72; 'Grant of Easement', 10; 'No-one's a Mystery', 12; 'Two Ghosts of Us', 12; *Time with Children*, 10; 'Why I Love Country Music', 10
thirtysomething, 165
Tin Men, 53–4
Tobacco Road (Caldwell), 94

Twain, Mark, 133
Tyler, Anne, 9, 53–72, 74, 75, 76, 90, 151; *The Accidental Tourist*, 42, 53, 54, 63, 64, 69–72, 76; *Celestial Navigation*, 54, 55–8; *Dinner at the Homesick Restaurant*, 54, 63, 64–8; *Searching for Caleb*, 54, 58–63

Uncle Vanya, 155
Updike, John, 27, 74, 75, 117, 159, 165

Vogue, 34

Walters, John, 53
Webster, Duncan, 10, 11, 12, 79, 87, 118, 130
Welty, Eudora, 45, 75, 93
Williams, Joy, 27, 45, 116, 124–31; *Breaking and Entering*, 131; 'Bromeliads', 127; *Escapes*, 127–31; 'Escapes', 126; 'The Little Winter', 127; 'The Lover', 125–26; 'Rot', 129–31; 'The Skater', 127–28; *Taking Care*, 124–27; 'Taking Care', 126; 'The Wedding', 124–25, 126; 'Winter Chemistry', 127, 128–29
Williams, Tennessee, 94
Winder, Robert, 50, 105
Wolfe, Tom, 90–1
Wolff, Tobias, 9, 10, 11, 30, 31, 116, 133–49; *Back in the World*, 133, 135; 'The Barracks Thief', 133, 141–44; 'Coming Attractions', 136; 'Desert Breakdown 1968', 139, 140; 'An Episode in the Life of Professor Brooke', 134, 137; 'Face to Face', 138–39, 140, 141; *Hunters in the Snow*, 133, 138; 'Hunters in the Snow', 141; 'In the Garden of the North American Martyrs', 138; 'Leviathan', 140; 'The Liar', 135–36, 148; 'Next Door', 139; 'Passengers', 140; 'The Poor Are Always With Us', 141; 'The Rich Brother', 135, 136, 140; 'Sister', 140, 141; 'Smokers', 137; 'Soldier's Joy', 141; *This Boy's Life*, 133, 135, 145–49
Wood, James, 45

Yardley, Jonathan, 76